Deleuze and Guattari

Continuum Studies in Continental Philosophy
Series Editor: James Fieser, University of Tennessee at Martin, USA

Continuum Studies in Continental Philosophy is a major monograph series from Continuum. The series features first-class scholarly research monographs across the field of Continental philosophy. Each work makes a major contribution to the field of philosophical research.

Adorno's Concept of Life, Alastair Morgan
Badiou and Derrida, Antonio Calcagno
Badiou, Balibar, Ranciere, Nicholas Hewlett
Deconstruction and Democracy, Alex Thomson
Deleuze and Guattari's Philosophy of History, Jay Lampert
Deleuze and Guattari: A Psychoanalytic Itinerary, Fadi Abou-Rihan
Deleuze and the Meaning of Life, Claire Colebrook
Deleuze and the Unconscious, Christian Kerslake
Derrida and Disinterest, Sean Gaston
Encountering Derrida, edited by Simon Morgan-Wortham and Allison Weiner
Foucault's Heidegger, Timothy Rayner
Heidegger and the Place of Ethics, Michael Lewis
Heidegger Beyond Deconstruction, Michael Lewis
Heidegger's Contributions to Philosophy, Jason Powell
Husserl's Phenomenology, Kevin Hermberg
The Irony of Heidegger, Andrew Haas
Levinas and Camus, Tal Sessler
Merleau-Ponty's Phenomenology, Kirk M. Besmer
The Philosophy of Exaggeration, Alexander Garcia Düttmann
Ricoeur and Lacan, Karl Simms
Sartre's Ethics of Engagement, T. Storm Heter
Sartre's Phenomenology, David Reisman
Who's Afraid of Deleuze and Guattari? Gregg Lambert

Deleuze and Guattari

A Psychoanalytic Itinerary

Fadi Abou-Rihan

continuum

Continuum International Publishing Group

The Tower Building
11 York Road
London SE1 7NX

80 Maiden Lane
Suite 704
New York NY 10038

www.continuumbooks.com

British Library Cataloguing-in-Publication Data
A catalogue record for this book is available from the British Library.

ISBN-13: PB: 978-1-4411-3778-4

Library of Congress Cataloguing-in-Publication Data
Abou-Rihan, Fadi.
Deleuze and Guattari: a psychoanalytic itinerary/Fadi Abou-Rihan.
p. cm.
Includes bibliographical references and index.

ISBN-13: 978-1-4411-3778-4 (PB)

1. Deleuze, Gilles, 1925–1995. 2. Guattari, Félix, 1930–1992.
3. Psychoanalysis. 4. Deleuze, Gilles, 1925–1995. Anti- Œdipe. I. Title.

B2430. D454A26 2008
194–dc22 2008013535

Typeset by Newgen Imaging Systems Pvt Ltd, Chennai, India
Printed and bound in Great Britain by Biddles Ltd, King's Lynn, Norfolk

For their gift of presence, I dedicate this book to Antonio Calcagno, Kathy Daymond, Margaret Huntley, François Lachance and Jeannelle Savona.

Contents

Preface

Most commentators have situated Deleuze and Guattari's *Anti-Oedipus* along two principal hermeneutic axes, the one historico-political, as an ethic grounded in the events of May 1968, and the other textual, as a Nietzschean reordering of Marx and Freud, ostensibly uncomfortable to both Marxists and Freudians. Very few indeed have seen fit to locate the text, and positively so, within a specifically psychoanalytic tradition. After all, the advocates of schizoanalysis consider the text a Medusa into whose face psychoanalysis cannot but stare and subsequently suffer the most abominable of deaths. And, to believe the few within the clinical circles that have actually bothered to read it, one would think *Anti-Oedipus* is, at best, a well-intentioned but thoroughly misguided flash in the pan. Both of these responses suffer from (1) a reading strategy that treats psychoanalysis and schizoanalysis as opposing paradigms caught up in a dispute over the so-called truth of the unconscious, and hence (2) an exclusive focus on the ways in which either paradigm can trap, conquer and/or discredit the other. While I do not wish to underestimate the critical legacy with which *Anti-Oedipus* has been rightly credited, I want to insist on a no less significant but much less manifest productive, psychoanalytic legacy that needs to be unravelled. To ignore that legacy is to wrest the text from its theoretical and practical matrix and reify its authors' richly ambivalent position.

My plan in the following pages is to reorganize the various components of the debate and show how, in underscoring the truly productive core of desire, Deleuze and Guattari remain fully committed to Freud's most singular discovery of an unconscious that is procedural and dynamic. I will show how *Anti-Oedipus* is not only a harsh and most insightful critique of the assimilationist vein in psychoanalysis, but that it is also, and more profoundly, a practice where the science of the unconscious is made to obey the laws it attributes to its object. The outcome here is nothing short of the 'becoming-unconscious' of psychoanalysis, a becoming that signals neither the repression nor the death of the practice but the transformation of its principles and procedures into those of its object. Psychoanalysis is no longer the subject that speaks of the unconscious; it is subject to it. Ostensibly, Deleuze and Guattari's anti-oedipal project is 'anti-' insofar as it ushers in a much needed moment of reflexivity where psychoanalytic theory and practice meet, where the theory is practised on itself, where the theory finds itself on the couch it has produced.

I want to track this anti-oedipal reflexivity alongside Nietzsche, Winnicott, Freud, Feynman, Bardi, Sophocles and Cixous. Along the way, I will unsettle the psychoanalytic axiom that pins identity onto a sexuality that is presumably always already tragic. I will rediscover a productive desire that belongs neither to subject nor to object but to the verb in its unfolding, to the verb as a gerund. I will conclude with a reformulation of the analytic process as an agile and resilient traversal, without design or resolution, in conflict and surprise.

Acknowledgements

Over the years, this text and I have been sustained by many. Among them are Fouad, Lily, Hania and Hani Abou-Rihan, Julie Allen, Chrys Bentley, Sam Bleiweiss, Michael Davey, Zeina Fawaz, John Keller, Brian Pronger, Haydar Sadek, Pat Skippon, Michelle Switzer and Peter Trnka. While some have remained, others, sadly, are no longer; to all, my deepest gratitude.

I also owe a debt of thanks to Elena Basile, Stephanie Bot, Deborah Britzman, Michelle Flax, Marlene Goldman, Camilla Mryglod, Craig Patterson, Lucy Potter, Scott Rayter, Douglas Robinson, Lindsay Shane, and all the other colleagues (clinical and academic) who participated in my *Anti-Oedipus* seminar, who attended the conferences at which I presented earlier chapter drafts, or with whom I had a chance to discuss my often less than coherent thoughts. Their generosity and patience helped shape much of what follows.

Chapter One

Nietzsche: by way of an introduction

Midway through his career, and as he was taking stock of his achievements so far, Freud declared he would gladly forego all claims to priority 'in the many instances in which laborious psychoanalytic investigation can merely confirm the truths which the philosopher recognized by intuition' ('On the History of the Psychoanalytic Movement', 73). The philosopher in question is none other than Friedrich Nietzsche and, among his 'intuited' truths, Freud will acknowledge the work of primeval relics in the dream (*The Interpretation of Dreams*, 700), the influence that affects exert on memory (*The Psychopathology of Everyday Life*, 198n1), and, most importantly, the 'impersonal' component of the psyche for which the '*es*' (the 'it' that is rendered sadly as 'id' in English) is a most deserving appellation ('The Ego and the Id', 362). Unfortunately, and as Freud went on to consolidate for psychoanalysis the status of a science and a treatment whose credibility and legitimacy, presumably, must leave little if any room for 'intuition', Nietzsche's presence in the clinical literature would become an 'embarrassment' ('An Autobiographical Study', 244) to the point where it had to be rendered virtually imperceptible.[1]

Interestingly, and rather than an inspiration for analytic understanding and insight, the philosopher is nowadays more likely to be deployed as the tool and justification for a critique of psychoanalysis and its basic principles. Witness, for instance, the great lengths to which many studies have gone in arguing how Deleuze and Guattari's so-called anti-psychoanalytic project is deeply embedded in a Nietzschean paradigm of man and world. In this context, one can follow a most useful trajectory from, among others, the early monographs of Vincent Descombes and Franco Rella, on to the analyses of Eugene Holland, and, most recently, to those of Monique David-Ménard.[2] The consensus among these and many other studies has been that, whether justifiable or not, it is Nietzsche's philosophy of difference and becoming that fuels the anti-oedipal project as a critique of psychoanalysis (qua theory, practice and institution) and as a positive and hopefully more accurate elaboration of the psyche's powers and possibilities.

In the following pages, I would like to pursue an approach that deviates, strategically at least, from the one adopted by these studies. Rather than tracking a conceptual debt or family resemblance, I want to explore the ties that link Deleuze and Guattari to their German predecessor from the point of view of the madness that permeates much of Nietzsche's text. It is in light of a madness that is advocated (as productive anachronism) and suffered (as stagnant hyper-conformity), a madness that is hence both a theoretical strategy and a lived experience, that I want to trace the connective lines which, almost a century later, led Deleuze and Guattari to their categories of desiring production, schizophrenic process and social delirium.

I want to deploy the doubled structure of this madness in order to highlight a Nietzschean psychology according to which subjects and agencies are defined by the relations they enter into with one another rather than by their qualities as discrete and enumerable entities. This psychology figures among the relations that define its objects and is consequently defined by them. This psychology is therefore implicated in the relationality it identifies. It is with this lens of necessary, and at times maddening, reflexivity in hand that my project will move through the texts and the strategies. At stake here is a reassessment of the mutually exclusive dyads subject/object, speech/silence and sanity/madness. These are the dyads that psychoanalysis has relied upon and reinforced in its understanding of the subject as a discrete entity that suffers the lack of an object, of desire as always already inscribed in the supposedly universal and immutable structures of language and of sanity as the opposite of the inchoate and, hence, the dangerously unintelligible.

Madness

Be it his or others', Nietzsche courted madness throughout his life. Fascination and dread rarely failed to accompany his utterances on the matter. Nietzsche thought madness a 'neurosis of health' (*BT*, Attempt at a Self-Criticism, #4[3]) by means of which an individual may ascend to the heights of tragedy; a 'rare and singular standard' (*GS*, #55) that is the shadow of a trait previously considered common but now re-emerging in a world where it has become 'strange, extraordinary' (*GS*, #10). In this sense then madness is the quintessential anachronism and the exception that never wants to become the rule, the undisciplined and arbitrary judgement that does not yield to the law of agreement (*GS*, #76). It is this madness that Nietzsche advances under his rubric of the free spirit and higher man, of the solitary 'improviser of life' (*GS*, #303) and 'actor of his own ideals' (*BGE*, #97). It is also this madness that the philosopher enacts through his aphoristic style. Indeed, the aphorism for Nietzsche is neither an argument that has been distilled down to its purest and most elegant, nor an element of a broader and more complex schema without which it is lost or stripped of meaning; it is the ceaselessly jarring exception that contradicts, questions and complicates, the exception that rarely admits to an adequate classification in a chronology or essence. It is in this sense that, in Nietzsche, the aphorism is the untimely (*unzeitgemäßen*) fragment that is inscribed in time but resolutely out of sync with its time.

However, and much like any other component of his thought, madness for Nietzsche is charged with more than one meaning and dynamic. Exceptional as it may often be, madness can also occupy the register of the mundane and the histrionic. It is that intoxication elicited through certain works of art and offered for the delectation of the 'wretched, exhausted, and sick' (*GS*, #89). In his later years, Nietzsche will judge Wagner as the clearest illustration of such a phenomenon: 'the problems [Wagner] presents on the stage – all of them problems of hysterics – the convulsive nature of his affects, his overexcited sensibility, his taste that required ever stronger spices, his instability which he dressed up as principles, not least of all the choices of his heroes and heroines . . . all of this taken together represents a profile of sickness that permits no further doubt. *Wagner est une névrose*' (*CW*, #5). Under this heading, madness is at times a planned respite, at others an entertaining diversion and at others still a momentary lapse in common sense. Throughout, the mediocre 'last man' condones this madness as long as it does not distract him from the repetitive life he seeks. In this sense, madness is the reward promised to all those who shall abide by the laws of the group. It is no longer an exception to the rule but an instrument that guarantees it (*BGE*, #145). In its exaggerated mode, this madness has also become the intended outcome of a senseless regimen of fasting, abstinence and isolation – in one word, denial – under the guise of which new laws are to be framed. It has become the rubble, and the rabble, that paves the way for martyrdom and sainthood, Christian or otherwise (*D*, #14).

These Nietzschean registers of madness are relational in two distinct ways. First, and whether exceptional or mundane, anachronistic or conformist, madness is not an isolated and static category; it is always identified and measured in the context of a surround that it either unsettles or confirms. Second, and inasmuch as each of the two registers defines itself in terms of a distinct set of guidelines and expectations, each also speaks the other as constitutive but subordinate, as the hapless opposite, qua pathology and/or threat, into which it cannot and must not lapse.

Ironically enough, and wittingly or not, Nietzsche himself managed to do precisely just that, to lapse into the one while speaking the other, to cross the border that separates them and in the process to expose its arbitrariness and conceit.

On the one hand, and in the words of Peter Sloterdijk, we have Nietzsche's 'infinitely consequential artistic and philosophical double-natured eloquence' (*Thinker on Stage*, 10), his ability to develop his talents – literary, philosophical and musical – not only side by side but also through one another. In the process of what Sloterdijk terms a 'centauric' development, Nietzsche's work has flooded the institutionalized bifurcations of discourse and his outpourings continue to elude whatever might contain and manage them under the aegises of this or that rubric of intellectual or cultural production. In his own fashion then, Sloterdijk has reiterated the by now familiar Deleuzian line that Nietzsche's brilliance is grounded in a text that is no more a signifier than a signified, in a text that is a play of forces that express something that cannot be codified ('Nomad Thought', 145–46).

Sloterdijk goes on to underscore a crucial precondition for Nietzsche's eloquence: his abandoning his imagined audience or at least his ceasing to be concerned with whether his actual audience understands or accepts him (*Thinker on Stage*, 10). Nietzsche of course, and as far as he was concerned, went much further than that. Rather than merely abandoning his audience, he frequently oscillated between misleading it, avoiding it and altogether pushing it away. His irreverent and equivocal pronouncements, his invariably original and often shockingly idiosyncratic retrieval of texts, characters and events, and, last but not least, his rejection of all that hinted at, much less advocated, the collective or democratic all rendered him inimical to the times' prevailing standards of equality, progress and accuracy. Ultimately, and if the philosopher had his way, neither he nor the precursors he acknowledged (Heraclitus and Spinoza for instance) nor the rare followers he anticipated would ever belong to a history or a taxonomy of ideas that could regulate, predict or disseminate their inner workings. This is not to suggest that Nietzsche pursued anonymity or indifference. On the contrary, he demanded a most peculiar type of recognition that is grounded in a logic of unremitting dis-identification, a logic that pre-empts familiarity and sympathy, let alone idealization. Evidently, Nietzsche had set for himself the task of philosophical madness.

On the other hand, there are, of course, the often invoked 11 final years in Nietzsche's life. Plagued by the dementia and paralysis typically associated with tertiary syphilis, the philosophical genius is now reduced to a helpless and barren volatility. His days are an unqualified childishness punctuated with the occasional outburst of animal-like rage. At this point, it is tempting to deploy such a pathology as a means for discrediting Nietzsche's thought, for arguing that the stage for the ultimate deterioration, in both health and meaning, had been set by a lifelong history of antisocial, hypo-manic, megalomaniacal and paranoid, not to mention physically debilitating, patterns that had left their unmistakable mark of insanity on his text. Alternatively, and as a way of countering this not so subtle *ad hominum*, one could insist on separating the work from the man, on arguing for and locating in the text an intellectual richness that is to be safeguarded from the offending if not, again but differently, embarrassing biographical particulars of its author. With both of these options, the emphasis on either life or work, on either body or text, investing in the one in order to discredit the other, remains fairly unequivocal. Invariably, the classic but tired split between a damning physicality and a redeeming thought is reinforced; the same mistaken assumption is deployed in order to sustain two differing and yet equally misguided verdicts.

As for Nietzsche himself, he hardly made any attempt to dismiss his afflictions as accidental to his project. On the contrary, the philosopher affirmed the debt he owed to his protracted illness time and again. While the 'free spirits' to whom he dedicated *Human All Too Human* were invented because he 'needed their company at the time, to be a good cheer in the midst of bad things (illness, isolation, foreignness, sloth, inactivity)' (*HH*, #2), *The Gay Science*, on the other hand, was a refined and convalescent cheerfulness that could not have obtained without the 'fickle health' and 'severe sickness' (*GS*, Preface, #3) that preceded and accompanied it. Furthermore, 'the perfect brightness and cheerfulness [Nietzsche writes], even exuberance of the spirit, reflected in [*Daybreak*], is compatible . . . not only with the most profound physiological weakness, but even with an excess of pain' (*EH*, I #1).

In insisting on such a pain as counterpoint, cause, or companion to his thought, Nietzsche did not consider himself an exception but an example of the philosopher whose task is to reconfigure the many kinds of physical health and sickness into spiritual form:

> We philosophers [he writes again] are not free to divide body from soul as the people do; we are even less free to divide soul from spirit. We are not thinking frogs, nor objectifying and registering mechanisms with their innards removed; constantly, we have to give birth to our thoughts out of our pain and, like mothers, endow them with all we have of blood, heart, fire, pleasure, passion, agony, conscience, fate, and catastrophe. (*GS*, Preface #3)

Perhaps the philosopher's commitment to laborious (re)generation and the last man's aspirations to martyrdom do intersect after all. Perhaps, structurally at least, there is much that still needs to be said regarding the link between a newborn infant and an old saint.

Body

Though in one respect metaphorical, Nietzsche's comments on pain and illness demand to be appreciated in their most literal moment as well. In fact, and however politically contentious it has become, the philosopher's insistence on an indissoluble unity between body and mind, his as well as anyone else's for that matter, remains one of the few central motifs recurring throughout his entire career. The body for Nietzsche is not a primordial and otherwise static materiality upon which the dramas of the affective, the ideological, or the scientific are to be staged; it is not a pre-existing field upon which various 'dynamic quanta' operate:

> Behind our thoughts and feelings, my brother, there stands a mighty ruler, an unknown sage – whose name is self. In your body he dwells; he is your body . . . The creative self created respect and contempt; it created pleasure and pain. The creative body created the spirit as a hand for its will. (*Z*, I, #4)[4]

For Nietzsche, art, science, religion and morality are but the most recent outward expressions and sublimations of the self's passion for play, exploration, subjection or classification (*WP*, #677). Take for instance the 'bold insanities' of metaphysics; they are most valuable for the historian and psychologist as 'hints or symptoms of the body' (*GS*, Preface #2). Metaphysics does not operate in the lofty realm of Idea or Spirit; it is produced by the body and belongs to it. As a 'symptom', it draws attention to that body, gives it a voice and interprets it. Metaphysics hence implicates itself in whatever order and value it assigns that body. Any philosophy that is based on an ossification or denial of its materiality, and hence any philosophy that has deluded itself into a so-called anaclitic relationship with a material base from which it once originated but which it has long since supposedly surpassed, is potentially doomed to a nihilistic self-destruction. Conversely, it is only a philosophy acutely aware of its corporeal determinants and willing to risk the hazards of its and their endless mutations that stands the chance of fulfilling the Nietzschean promise of madness.

Without lapsing into the language of either causality or dialectic, one may then speak of a thought and a body enfolding, triggering, contaminating or reverberating in one another. One may then speak not so much of a text, a context and a theory that interprets or justifies them, but of a complex and malleable matrix that incorporates all three components and defines them in terms of their often-unmediated relations of power to one another (*WP*, #89, #635).[5] Ultimately for Nietzsche,

> coming to know means 'to place oneself in a conditional relation to something'; to feel oneself conditioned by something and oneself to condition it – it is therefore under all circumstances establishing, denoting and making-conscious of conditions (not forthcoming entities, things, what is 'in-itself'). (*WP*, #555)

The world we know is a world of conditional relations and not of objects. Stripped of such relations, it and our ability to know it cease to exist. This is one expression of an all-encompassing Nietzschean cosmology, of a world that we have subdivided and classified into 'subjects', 'objects', 'facts', 'events', 'species' and 'structures'. That such manoeuvres have proven themselves quite useful, and sometimes even necessary, is not at issue. What is often overlooked however is the fact that they constitute but 'a language of signs', 'a fiction' and 'a conceit' (*WP*, #676) reflecting a world 'unspeakably' greater than any representation we might accord it (*WP*, #674).[6]

That Nietzsche's is a world beyond representation has little to do with the non-verbal that psychoanalysis has often rendered as pre-verbal (read inchoate, schizophrenic even). Lacan's characterization of the *infans* or Klein's diagnosis of concrete thinking are classic on this score.[7] The entry into language (contra speech, for the Lacanians) and the capacity for symbolic representation (contra symbolic equation, for the Kleinians) are the marks of a psyche that has acquired the ability and, correspondingly, the responsibility to re-present, which is to say to make present again but differently, a phallus or a mother that will henceforth be tolerated in their absences. Language then is no simple communicative tool; it is both a faculty the individual must attain and a faculty that is in the service of that individual's growth. This is axiomatic for psychoanalysis as a 'talking cure'. The re-presentation is also the interpretation that will bridge the gap between what is conscious and what is unconscious, what is and what was or is no longer, what is inside and what is outside. Invariably here, language is brought to bear on discrete entities, whether organic or structural. Nietzsche for his part was concerned much less with drives, objects and demarcations and more with relations and processes. It is for this reason that he chose to forego the logic of a subject and instead invoked the impersonal note of an 'it' that is beyond speech, much as Freud will soon after qualify as silent the unconscious work of dreams and the dynamics of mourning for instance. That such phenomena are silent does not imply that they are inchoate.

Production

When pressed, Nietzsche will describe his 'unspeakable' world in terms that, initially at least, might evoke visions of eternal ecstasy and/or intractable horror. This is the world of the 'will to power', the world that is a

> monster of energy, without beginning, without end; a firm, iron magnitude of force that does not grow bigger or smaller, that does not expend itself but only transforms itself; a sea of forces flowing and rushing together, eternally changing, eternally flooding back, with tremendous years of recurrence, with an ebb and a flood of its forms. (*WP*, #1067)

Nietzsche will then go on to clarify that this is also the 'Dionysian world of the eternally self-creating, the eternally self-destroying, [a] mystery world of the twofold voluptuous delight . . . "beyond good and evil", without goal, unless the joy of the circle is itself a goal, without will, unless a ring feels good will toward itself' (*WP*, #1067).

This is the world that, in one respect at least, could not be any farther from the unconscious that most branches of psychoanalysis have captured. It is the world that knows nothing of stages and aims, positions and resolutions, structures and registers; it is the world of transformation, of creation and destruction. This is the world of desiring-production with which Deleuze and Guattari will confront their readers from the opening lines of their *Anti-Oedipus* 'it is at work everywhere, functioning smoothly at times, at other times in fits and starts' (3) and all the way till the book's concluding declaration that it is 'always and already complete as it proceeds, and as long as it proceeds' (382). In the chapters that follow, we shall see how this world is precisely the world of the unconscious as a primary process and hence as a way of thinking that psychoanalysis has articulated, in spite of its scientific aspirations and therapeutic investments.

At this point, we may wish to interrupt Nietzsche, the man and the text, and request a modicum of consistency: is this latest conception of the world itself not to be considered as yet another fiction? The 'dynamic quanta' hypothesized, the 'will to power' posited and the 'eternal recurrence' advocated, must these not be implicated in the same logic of usefulness and conceit attributed to all the other philosophies and sciences? To answer this question in the affirmative should prove shocking neither to many of Nietzsche's readers nor, for that matter, to Nietzsche himself. On the side of the readers, Klossowski, for instance, showed quite eloquently how eternal recurrence is nothing but a 'willed error' (*Un si funeste désire*, 217) and a 'simulacrum of a doctrine' (226), and Deleuze, picking up on Klossowski's point, went on to argue the untruth of eternal recurrence as the motor of Nietzsche's subversion of the philosophical dualities original–copy, good–evil, body–spirit (*The Logic of Sense*, 253–66).

On the side of Nietzsche, a provisional plan for a book entitled 'The Eternal Recurrence', after his most widely debated 'doctrine', identifies the thought's place in his philosophical vision as merely a mid-point. The plan highlights sections of the book dealing not only with the thought's consequences and the means of enduring it but also with the means of disposing of it (*WP*, #1057). That such a plan exists suggests that, at least as far as Nietzsche was concerned, the thoughts of eternal recurrence and, by extension, of will to power are not so much theories that must be preserved and defended in the name of a universal truth but instead the outcomes of his philosophical experiments and, potentially, the tools that will be deployed in the service of future experiments that may very well produce further outcomes that have little or nothing to do with either return or will.

Life had once taught Zarathustra that '[w]hatever I create and however much I love it – soon I must oppose it and my love' (*Z*, II, 12). The philosopher rids the things he fashions of the all-too-common language of deification, immutability and universality; he will treat them irreverently; he will push them aside by 'flooding' or 'extinguishing' their character (*GS*, #361); he will dissolve their unity and coherence and in the process expose their false nature. This he does not in the service of a gratuitous or self-perpetuating destructiveness but as part of the process of philosophizing, of thinking, of creating: 'we who think and feel at the same time are those who really continually fashion something that had not been there before; the whole eternally growing world of valuations, colors, accents, perspectives, scales, affirmations, and negations' (*GS*, #301). What Nietzsche is privileging here has nothing to do with either producer or product but with production itself.

Indeed, production, philosophical or otherwise, is not structured according to the standards of an abstract and consistent truth; its outcome is not an a-historical and hence eternally deferred constant to which one can appeal as either an ontological justification or an ethical judgement that an impossible future will undoubtedly pass on an incomplete present. Such a constant is a fetish. The philosopher is the first to recognize his cosmology as a transitory product in the present; it is charged with the difficult task of simultaneously satisfying the moment's exigencies while undermining its fixity and necessity. The philosophical product challenges its time rather than colludes with it; as a product of its time, it is hence challenging and undermining of itself as well. It is always making itself other; it is un-self-timely. The quintessential relationship between the philosopher as producer and the philosophy as product will always involve betrayal as well as fidelity. It is worth keeping in mind here that this relationship's doubled nature has little to do with the ambivalence psychoanalysis has identified at the core of the subject's encounter with an object, with, in other words, the long-standing clinical disposition toward the experiences of love and hate as inevitably soldered to one another. Here, neither the producer nor the product is key; Nietzsche underscores what the relationship between the two does rather than what it is; his focus is on that relationship's ability to produce rather than on its subject's hoped for capacity to tolerate or its object's inherent condition to frustrate and satisfy.

Representation

The issue at this point becomes one of deploying Nietzsche's world of productive relations, in both its content and status as a representation, for appreciating the philosopher's final collapse into insanity. The currency of syphilis as the key to Nietzsche's pathology, and in a sense the physiological culprit, may be useful for some purposes but, historically at least, it is far from being conclusive. Moreover, it is misleading in the context of the present thoughts since it operates at the level of a crude and one-dimensional causal relationship between body and mind. The task at this point instead is to multiply the connections and in the process to rid them of their exclusively unidirectional fixity.

In the final remark of her study on Nietzsche and metaphor, Sarah Kofman postulates that

> to be fully metaphorical, or 'proper', a writing would have to invent a unique code, an impossible original language containing evaluations which had never taken place. A minimum of writing, speaking, and making oneself heard, despite being misheard – of vulgarising oneself ever

> so slightly – is an ineluctable fate; otherwise, one falls into silence and/or madness. (*Nietzsche and Metaphor,* 119)

Here, Kofman captures the spirit of Nietzsche's predicament with respect to both the world and the knowledge one can have of it. However, her alternatives – the mad, the vulgarized, and the silent – are misleadingly disjunctive. In fact, they are all present in Nietzsche, not as the discreet and sequential steps of his career as it met, or failed to meet, with its audiences and interlocutors, but as that career's simultaneous and overdetermined moments. The madness Nietzsche endured was of at least two kinds: the anachronistically creating and the ascetically stagnating. The silence he lived was as much the effect of a long-standing mistrust as it was the symptom of the inherently unspeakable presence he lived. Speech was not an option but a necessity that betrayed its own limit just as it suffered the betrayal of its vulgarizing speaker and audience.

Invariably, Nietzsche defied the purity of the exclusive either/or (subject/object, silence/speech, madness/sanity) not by exclusion but by inclusion. His life and text do not so much stake out a middle ground or territory hitherto outlawed by the logic of discrete limits. For, if the philosopher had done only that, he would have merely substituted one exclusive disjunction (*either* this *or* that limit) with another (*either* this or that limit *or* that which lies in between the two); he would have thus left the structure of exclusivity and all of its attendant by-products perfectly intact. Instead, Nietzsche affirms not only the in-between but also the so-called limits that, up until now, one could either avoid or hope to approximate. In the process of such a double affirmation however, the purity of these limits is unsettled and the network of forces that sustains the tension and distance between them as supposedly distinct opposites is released. Each limit is hence propelled on to the arena of these forces and made to participate in that which it had previously only contained. It is obliterated only insofar as it is a limit. It no longer carries the task of origin, ideal, fate or prohibition. It is simply one among the many forces whose interactions produce the body and the world as matrix.

In Nietzsche, then, the subject that is plagued by indomitable lack and the object that is invested with absolute satisfaction do not vanish; both are reorganized as but two of the many components in a complex process of production in which they will participate as both agents and effects. Speech and silence are no longer the avoidable dangers or future-deferrable ideals but the constitutive elements of the philosopher's and the text's present and ineluctable condition just as much as the vulgarizing metaphor has always been. Finally, sanity and madness are much less states of being than the qualities of the relations by which subjects, objects and texts are continually produced. Opposition is hence neither denied nor erased; it is transformed from a mutually exclusive disjunction into a malleable and productive connection.

Zarathustra again: 'It is a distinction to have many virtues, but a hard lot; and many have gone into the desert and taken their lives because they wearied of being the battle and battlefield of virtues' (*Z*, I #5). Fortunately or not for Nietzsche, it is not simply a consciously willed strategy of retreat or a devastating physiological condition that marked the end of his career; rather, it was his ability to occupy what lies on both sides of the divide between speech and silence, sanity and madness, which is to say his ability to live the relations that cross that divide and hence suffer the battles it produces. This ability had been at work throughout most of his texts. Had his spirit finally grown wary and tired of such crossings? As much as it may tell of a pathologically manic organization, the evidence also points to an overabundant creativity which, in its final year, bequeathed us four of the philosopher's most eloquent and cruelly insightful manuscripts,[8] as well as copious notes for a magnum opus that was to revaluate the major landmarks of Western history and culture. Still, and after all, behind, underneath and all around such outcomes lies the matrix of forces of which creativity is but one symptom. To ignore the others is to render Nietzsche a grave injustice, not so much in the form of a partial, and hence inaccurate, diagnostic portrait of his life on which we, as his supposed 'clinicians' or 'interpreters', are expected to report, but as a failure to recognize the profoundly original grouping of words and events of which he was both clinician and interpreter.

A greater appreciation of, and perhaps even commitment to, the geography of Nietzsche's madness, the topo-dynamic qualities of the matrix within which his life and work are to be, in some ways at least, coded, registered and operated – that is what is called for at this point. In turn, this appreciation itself needs to be located within the broader matrix of readings and uses triggered by the Nietzsche phenomenon. That, in its first century, such a matrix has turned into an industry, both military/fascistic and intellectual/academic, is not much of a coincidence. One could easily trace its polarities to the conflictual, indeed maddening, quality of a text whose principal character (Zarathustra/Nietzsche) stands as the quintessential metaphor of the double bind. 'Follow me by not following me' and 'be original, like me;' these are the maddening demands of a pedagogue caught up in the inner workings of his own teaching. These are also the maddening demands that have been invested with the power to unleash an ambivalence that has been held responsible for everything from a severe adult psychopathology, as with Bateson in his 'Towards a Theory of Schizophrenia', to a liberatory separation of the real from the necessary, of experience from dogma, as with Deleuze and Guattari in their *Anti-Oedipus*.

Be that as it may, both the phenomenon and its repercussions – the latter considered in all of their varieties and as a whole – witness to the return of the same madness, complexity and breadth. That the twentieth century ought to be known as, among other things, Nietzschean is hardly a controversial proposition. The conceptual and political uses the philosopher's writings have been made to serve remain among the most trenchant in human history. The academic investments in studies delineating his impact on this or that movement or persona continue to yield their expected interest. Currently, and much more curiously and perhaps even significantly, it is the hypotheses of the richest and most abstract cluster of sciences (quantum gravity, network theory and even neuroscience) that seem to echo the philosopher's principal insight that it is conditional relations and processes rather than objects per se that define the nature and scope of knowledge.

Reflexivity

As for psychoanalysis, Freud's embarrassment notwithstanding, there is much to Nietzsche, or at least to Nietzsche as I have introduced him, that still needs to be recognized and harnessed. Aside from such notions as a body ego or an 'impersonal' unconscious, I am also interested in Nietzsche's redefinition of knowledge as the effect of a process whereby one places oneself 'in a conditional relation to something' (*WP*, #555). This redefinition is much too close to the psychoanalytic understanding and use of the clinical transference for it to be a coincidence or a fantasy. However, and as a process whose aim is the making-conscious of 'conditions' rather than of entities, structures, or drives (*WP*, #555), this Nietzschean knowledge undermines the status that representation has come to occupy in the psychoanalytic field. As a talking cure, psychoanalysis is a working through instead of a working out only because it privileges in language its ability to re-present the structure and status of a yet unspoken desire. In so doing, it confines that desire, and by extension the relationship between subject and object, to the polarities of presence and absence, production and consumption, satisfaction and frustration. It struggles against these polarities and hopes to make them at the very least tolerable. Put differently, psychoanalysis speaks the unconscious so that it may contain it. Consequently, the practice finds that it can speak the unconscious only insofar as it is not subject to it, only insofar as it has immunized itself (as a theory) to the laws and dynamics of that of which it speaks (as a primary process).

The fact that the line between containment and confinement is often a very fine one indeed has not been lost on most psychoanalytic schools. However, the notion that the divide between subject and object, or self and other, can be bridged only through representational means remains for many the founding principle of the practice. For Nietzsche, representation is not the only, and hardly the most important, relational modality that obtains between subject and object. To know something is, again, to feel oneself conditioned by it. This conditioning is not a means toward a future epistemological gain; it is itself the knowledge. According to Nietzsche then, a theory must be conditioned by its object and implicated by the dynamics it ascribes to that object. From this perspective, and as a 'making-conscious', psychoanalysis needs to undergo a 'becoming-unconscious' in order for it to be truly a theory of the psyche in all of its layers and permutations. Short of such a becoming, and for better or for worse, psychoanalysis will remain trapped in the logic that fuels the dilemmas and dramas of such polarities as theory/practice and metapsychology/experience.

When psychoanalysis (rather than simply the individuals that participate in it) thinks itself not only as the disciplinary subject that speaks of the unconscious by means of abstractions and interventions but also as the utterance that is subject to the unconscious and its procedures, when, in other words, psychoanalysis lies down on the couch it has constructed and participates in free association, play or full speech – call it what you will, – all the while dreaming, slipping, emoting, fantasizing, then, and only then, will it, as a theory and a practice, disengage itself from the bias that invests representation with necessity, desire with lack, and madness with ineffability. Herein lies Nietzsche's truly maddening challenge to psychoanalysis. Herein also lies Deleuze and Guattari's equally maddening contribution.

Chapter Two

Winnicott: the psychoanalytic family

As a science of the psyche, psychoanalysis unfolds in the context of a relationship between two individuals, a relationship whose object is the unconscious and whose aim is truth. The fact that this relationship is effectively 'therapeutic' in nature and that much of what takes place within its frame is shaped by affects and phantasies[9] in no way lessen its investment in a theory and a science of the mind. The goal of the psychoanalytic experience has been widely debated and the concern with whether it is research and knowledge or the alleviation of suffering that ought to be its principal clinical focus has been a constant ever since the discipline's earliest days.[10] On the one hand, it is on the basis of its commitment to the truth of the unconscious, of, in other words, to setting for itself the task of making explicit the fact and quality of that unconscious in as accurate and rigorous a way as it possibly can, that psychoanalysis has claimed for itself the status of a veritable science and an effective intervention rather than a mundane or passing 'feel better' strategy. Yet, and on the other hand, it is also on the basis of the therapeutic experience as a very carefully conceived 'experiment' with its own protocols and procedures that psychoanalysis as a science has actually accrued its legitimacy. One would think that the goals of research and treatment must forever struggle against, repress or, at best, suffer the humiliation of needing one another.

Generally, the terms of this debate have been defined under the heading of a fairly classic understanding of knowledge as the product of a subject's thought and observation, as the set of unbiased (read: external and static) principles and techniques that must lend themselves to a number of different uses once the experiments have been concluded and the hypotheses verified. More fundamentally, however, knowledge here is the manifest representation a subject makes for itself of the object that it is not; it is the subject's way of reconstituting the object as internal and acquired rather than as other.[11] It is therefore a tool that allows the subject to bridge a distance and negotiate an absence. Ultimately then, knowledge is the third to a segment of a line connecting two entities that would otherwise remain flat and one-dimensional. In this light, psychoanalysis is an instantiation of such a third; it is the knowledge that a subject can acquire of that most dynamic and elusive of 'others' – its unconscious.

As I have suggested in the previous chapter, Nietzsche's challenge to this classic conception of knowledge involves reconfiguring the very structure that upholds the division and tension between subject and object, observer and observed. Nietzsche judged the elements that constitute the sets of opposites, limits and/or dyads as 'inaccurate' and 'useless' only insofar as they make an appeal to a knowledge and an aim that pretend to lie outside the actual classifications and exclusions. Put differently, and rather than forcing it *onto* the real, as much of science and philosophy have attempted before him, Nietzsche forces knowledge (whether a priori reason or empirical observation) *into* the real; he engages it in its own strategies and subjects it to the rules it presumably uncovers in its objects. Nietzsche does not rid reason or evidence of their relevance; he, in fact, makes them more real and hence, surprisingly, more relevant. Rather than a third that is the outcome or consequence of a pre-existing subject–object couplet, Nietzsche's knowledge reflects back on itself; it is a founding relationship that produces and directs subject and object, as they in turn condition it; it is a knowledge that is always already the object of its own enquiry and analysis.

In one respect at least, psychoanalysis has been acutely aware of this Nietzschean dynamic; it has taken it up as one of its major points of concern and gone on to deploy it as a principal clinical strategy. Indeed, and whether it is an intersubjective field or an exchange between the transference and the counter-transference, the conditioning fuels the clinical situation and shapes its participants. This, in fact, is how psychoanalysis has often set itself apart from all the other psychotherapeutic modalities. However, and whereas Nietzsche understood the knowledge and the conditioning as synchronous with the dyad in which they occur, psychoanalysis has generally insisted on distinguishing knowledge as either an outcome of or a requirement for the encounter between analyst and analysand, once, presumably, the conditioning has been identified and worked through. It is for this reason that knowledge has come to be seen by some psychoanalysts as hindered by a series of distorting demands and expectations that ought to be resolved, by others as furthered by a revitalizing site of free associations that deserves to be fostered and by others still as a presupposed but initially obscured structural reference without which the analytic dyad would not be possible.

As a science, psychoanalysis has assumed the responsibility of subjecting its formulations to constant scrutiny. From Freud's earliest revisions and all the way to the most recent investments in evidence-based research,[12] the discipline has insisted that its practitioners abide by some of the strictest and most time-consuming levels of commitment to 'disinterested' scientific accuracy and therapeutic efficacy. However, and by that same token, psychoanalysis the science cannot but live a passion for the unconscious that is its object; it cannot but hold a fascination with that object's inner dynamics and a curiosity toward its transformations,[13] How could it do otherwise? As a passion, however, psychoanalysis has been less than immune to its own set of conflicting and 'not quite scientific' pressures and aims. Among these we can count the discipline's struggles for survival, legitimacy and regeneration, not to mention its strivings for mastery over its institutional subjects as well as its clinical subject matter. As the practice has resorted to tolerate, sublimate and sometimes even repress its less than measured ambitions and inconsistencies, its detractors have often deployed them in the service of, sadly, some of the cruder and less insightful attacks.[14]

When genuine and studied, the debates around the validity and so-called accuracy of the psychoanalytic apparatus are not without their merit; they will no doubt continue to capture much energy and yield important insights. In this chapter, I would like to concentrate instead on the way psychoanalysis as a whole has so far negotiated the tension it suffers as it simultaneously struggles to consolidate its status as a science while it lives its basic nature as a passion.[15] My concern is much less with the ideological biases and projections of any particular school of thought or therapeutic orientation and lesser still with the clinical distortions and/or ramifications of any single clinician's counter-transferential limits and liabilities. Rather, it is the assumptions the discipline has deployed in understanding desire as its object, approach, and task that I am most interested in. I want to show how these assumptions have forced the dominant epistemological structure that demarcates subject from object and regulates their relation in terms of acquisition onto the realm of desire.

It seems to me that the psychoanalytic project has chosen to resolve its conflicted nature as both a science and a passion through a mechanism of duplication rather than one of reflexivity. It has deployed the scientific model of the triad subject–object-knowledge as the standard for understanding desire and its passions in terms of a lack that is henceforth regulated by its own triadic structure of subject–object-satisfaction. Obviously, psychoanalysis ought not be held culpable for a manoeuvre whose history extends back to the earliest moments in the Western tradition, both philosophical and scientific. However, and as the discipline that is the most intimately cognizant of the psyche's drives and dynamics, psychoanalysis enjoys the privilege, if not the responsibility, to uncover the structural biases and limitations of this tradition. Instead, it has opted not only to collude with but, and as I will show in following pages, also to contribute its own set of tools that will further extend that venerable tradition's reach into the very workings of its object.

Roughly, I want to show how the psychoanalytic passion for knowledge has somehow exempted itself from the status of a passion, how, in other words, knowledge has been, yet again, all too eager to, as Nietzsche put it, 'condition' the desire that is its object without allowing itself to be conditioned, and subsequently enriched, by it. In my treatment, I do not wish to make an appeal to any of the day's cultural or political sensibilities nor do I wish to fault psychoanalysis for having betrayed this or that ideological currency. Instead, and in the spirit of Nietzschean reflexivity, I want to deploy the standards that are strictly those of analytic enquiry itself. I want to show how, once it holds itself as object of its own mode of study, psychoanalysis cannot but uncover a compulsion to repeat, to duplicate without tolerance for the slightest deviation, to, effectively, fulfill the strictest standards of 'scientific' consistency in the service of a norm it must itself judge as most disturbing. The norm I will expose is that of reproduction in its most rudimentary physiological terms. I will show how psychoanalysis privileges that most 'scientific' of facts, the need for a species to duplicate itself in order to maintain its very existence, as the psychological standard of health by which all desire is to be categorized and assessed. In its appeal to an overriding biology, psychoanalysis undermines its own legitimacy as a discipline whose purview is the extra-physiological and whose object is precisely that which cannot be explained in terms of biology alone.

Put differently, I want to argue that psychoanalysis has trapped desire within the norms of biological reproduction and then gone on to institute fairly narrow standards of gender identification as defining guidelines in matters of both process and aim. Indeed, much of the psychoanalytic tradition has been burdened by its self-imposed prescription that the psychoanalyst must function as a masculine/fatherly source of truth and discipline and/or a feminine/motherly seat of nurture and safety – presumably, the source and/or seat the analysand had previously lacked. Ironically, and rather than the epigone of psychological health, the psychoanalyst that emerges out of this schema is an individual trapped in the logics of fetishism and melancholia, the same logics that psychoanalysis itself has repeatedly marked as pathological.[16]

I will deploy the work of D. W. Winnicott as a prime illustration of this dynamic. Indeed, it is Winnicott who is the most thematically relevant here since his project has sought to incorporate both poles of the gender dyad and their corresponding clinical adaptations. In exposing the limits and contradictions of the psychoanalyst-as-parent metaphor, I want to set the stage for the much-needed disruption of the discipline's uncritical projection of biology onto clinic, of fact onto phantasy, and of repetition onto desire. I believe that this disruption cannot be accomplished through a mere broadening or even problematizing of the categories of gender as many, mostly feminist, readers of psychoanalysis have suggested.[17] The disruption must involve a reformulation of the very definition of desire outside the frame of lack and of psychoanalysis outside the metaphor of re-parenting. This is where I find Deleuze and Guattari's deployment of the anti-oedipal notions of 'desiring machines' and 'bodies without organs' as a means of ridding psychoanalysis of any and all familial connotations most useful. I shall treat of this deployment, its metapsychological implications, and its clinical usefulness in the coming chapters.

In the meantime, the objection may be raised that the projects of Freud, Lacan or even Klein would have been more obvious choices than Winnicott's since this, after all, is a study of Deleuze and Guattari's texts and theories. Presumably, the philosopher and the psychoanalyst would have had little time, and even less patience, for anyone other than the figures already well established within the French psychoanalytic circles of the 1960s and 70s. However, while I believe that this or any other study for that matter must bear in mind the timeline of Deleuze and Guattari's backgrounds and preoccupations, it must not be limited by it. Ultimately, my project here is not simply a chronological account or a conceptual genealogy; I do not wish to retrieve Deleuze and Guattari's interventions only to have to return them cleaner and shinier to their so-called 'proper' places on the shelves of intellectual history. My investment is pragmatic as much as it is theoretical and my overall plan is to reassess these interventions and to deploy them with respect to some of the dynamics faced by the philosophers and psychoanalysts of today.

Grafts

Be it the austere father with whom and against whom the oedipal drama is to be completed or the empathic mother remedying infancy and early childhood deficits of nurture, the parental fallacy continues to be one of the most persistent and striking elements in psychoanalytic practice. This fallacy is persistent in its quasi-universality and striking in the uncritical support it has managed to accrue. Indeed, and with the notable exception of some of those working in the Lacanian and relational fields, the endorsement of the parental model as a marker of sound clinical practice has substituted the dynamic unconscious and its primary process as the principle through which the psychoanalytic profession has come to identify and unify itself. In spite of their differences with the ego-psychological paradigm upon which that arbiter of professional standards was founded, revisionists and so-called dissidents have been able to hold on to their presence within the International Psychoanalytical Association (IPA) not so much because of their allegiance to first principles regarding the structure and workings of the psyche but because of their endorsement of a mechanism whereby the parental stance is grafted onto both the institutional and the clinical.

Institutionally, this grafting has produced a hierarchy – the IPA – that is now fully grown into the status of what could be best described as a hermaphroditic' parent. The IPA is indeed the father who struggles to arrogate for himself the sole right to identify and police the genealogical lines of access and exclusion with respect to 'psychoanalysis' as a mode of enquiry and a professional designation. The association is also the mother who has assumed the responsibility of providing for her offspring's clinical and political sustenance through various mechanisms of representation and referral. In contrast to the image that the IPA has constructed of itself as the epitome of oedipal order and maturity, this grafting has also precipitated the growth of societies and institutes outside the fold that, not coincidentally, have often operated with a number of tropes and models other than the parental.

Clinically, the insistence on a parental schema and its attendant hierarchies of adult and child has served to reinforce a divide between an expert doctor and a hapless patient in matters of diagnosis, treatment, and health. This is the divide that psychoanalysis has carried over from its nineteenth century medical roots and with which it has constantly struggled. In a parallel mode, the parental schema has helped consolidate an understanding of psychopathology as a stagnation or a regression in the individual's temporal journey from primary, childish or archaic defences and coping mechanisms to more mature modes of organization of self and/or relations to others. Indeed, this has become axiomatic. Whether it is framed in terms of conflict or deficit, or a combination thereof, the cause of the psychological stagnation is located in a disruption in the individual's earliest relations with his or her primary caregivers. Under the banner of genital love, ego autonomy, the depressive position or an integrated self, health is posited invariably as a culminating 'adult' synthesis and with it are articulated not only the aims but also the modes and stages of analytic inquiry. In such a context, analysis is held up as that process by which a modified and healthier repetition of the original development is pursued, as, in other words, the process by which the analysand can become the adult he or she would have become but for the disruptions. All of this is, of course, contingent on the participation, facilitation and, effectively, supervision of an analyst who has already been qualified in matters of adulthood, parenting and care.

As the stage upon which this health-inducing repetition unfolds, the clinical transference is expected to absorb as many features of the pathology as it can bear and, in so doing, to allow for that pathology's re-emergence and possible treatment in an environment whose safety and robustness are guaranteed by the person of the healthy psychoanalyst. I want to defer for the future chapters a more thorough treatment of the questions and complications surrounding the primacy of this particular understanding of the transference as catalyst and vehicle of analytic work. For now, and while I obviously, do acknowledge the preponderance of an analysand's parental phantasies and their accompanying demands on the person of the psychoanalyst, I would like to highlight the fallacious nature of a practice that measures the worth, efficiency and goal of the psychoanalyst's position in terms of his or her supposedly appropriate functioning as mother and/or father. I want to argue that, in ascribing to the psychoanalyst the status of parent, such a practice not only fuels an un-worked through counter-transferential parental phantasy, it also bolsters parenting as a measure of health and, as a consequence, elevates reproduction from the status of a biological event to that of a psychological commandment: *Thou shall multiply.* In so doing, it conversely demotes anything other than a reproductive genital sexuality, as that which is in violation of said imperative, to the status of pathology. Ultimately, the parental counter-transference fuels a version of the psychoanalytic process by means of which desire is reduced, yet again, to a natural compulsion to reproduce, to consume only so that it may reproduce, and, ostensibly, to encounter the other as, primarily, a potential object of consumption and hence as a means toward reproduction.

Enters here Donald W. Winnicott whose work abounds with parental metaphors. According to Winnicott, the psychoanalyst must alternate quietly and deftly between the fatherly source of truth and discipline and the motherly seat of comfort and safety. My impression is that, not surprisingly, the metaphoric richness of Winnicott's work compensates for a paucity that is both theoretical and clinical. As will become clear soon enough, this paucity is made manifest most vividly by the Winnicottian psychoanalyst's oscillation between, on the one hand, the role of the mature adult who is circuitously the cause and product of health and, on the other hand, the role of the self-berating healer for whom every impasse is testimony to his or her empathic ineptitude. Unwittingly, Winnicott confines his psychoanalyst to the clinical positions that Freud before him had attributed to, respectively, the disavowing fetishist and the rhythmically monotonous melancholic.

Winnicott occupies a rare and most peculiar position in the history of psychoanalysis for he was the successor to one and the progenitor to the other of the two principal schools that have sustained the psychoanalyst-as-parent metaphor: Ego Psychology, with its investment in the authority and infallibility of the father, and Self Psychology, with its over-valuation of the mother's ability to provide and care. My intent in what follows is not to exhaust Winnicott's contributions for there is much in them that I find particularly useful, especially, and as I will argue in the final chapter, with regard to his categories of play and transitionality. My intent is not to caricature Winnicott's work either; I would like to stretch some of his key theoretical assumptions to their limit and, in so doing, to measure the extent of their malleability and to locate the points at which they cannot but break. Consider this then a stress test, a stress test whose impetus and mode lies in the as yet unresolved ambiguities of the intersection between the moments of counter-transference and therapeutic action.

Mother

Winnicott's most often quoted maxim 'there is no such thing as a baby' ('The Theory of The Parent–Infant Relationship', 39n1) attempts to capture the field of object relations crucial for analytic work. Unfortunately, such a maxim remains stuck, and stubbornly so, in a dyadic position that does not, and indeed cannot, account for the third – to wit, the structure that defines the dyad, sets its parameters, identifies its goals and prescribes its functions. The tie between mother and infant does not exist in a structural vacuum. This tie is anaclitic in nature; it serves to establish for the baby a link and an opposition between a physiological need and a libidinal drive. Both need and drive are not only directed toward an external object (the mother's breast for instance) for their satisfaction, they are moreover defined by that directionality. True enough, there is no such thing as a baby in the sense that a baby's presence is always already contingent upon that of a mother or someone fulfilling a motherly function of sorts. Equally true is the fact that there is no such thing as a mother; this is so not only in her role as a dyadic compliment to her baby but also as the one whose presence is always already contingent upon that of a set of cultural, historical, legal and communicative structures in matters of kinship and exchange. Indeed, and if a baby cannot exist without its mother, a mother cannot exist not only without a baby but, and much more crucially, without the structures that will allow her to identify, prioritize and minister to that baby's needs, that, in other words, will allow her to define and evaluate herself as a 'good enough' mother in an extra-physiological sense.

If one is to follow Winnicott in his move away from his time's commitment to Freud's atomistic theory of the human psyche and toward much more complex and overdetermined networks of interpersonal relations, one must also move away from a simplistic two-person psychology that remains oblivious to that third which allows the 'two' to be counted and made to communicate. By the 'third', I am not referring to what has become known as the 'analytic third' in the literature, e.g. the institutional, juridical and professional standards that are ever present in the clinical setting; nor am I referring to that 'third' that Thomas Ogden elaborated in his rereading of Winnicott's transitional space as the critical outcome of the encounter between mother and infant, analyst and analysand.[18] By the 'third', I am referring rather to that grid of which these factors are only symptoms and/ or effects, to that grid which precedes, underlies and mediates any and all communication. In eliding this third, the Winnicottian insistence on the maternal metaphor substitutes one problematic essence (the structural model) with another (the mutually satisfying mother–infant relationship), one unfounded therapeutic goal (a strong, balanced and resourceful ego in matters of conflict resolution) with another (a capacity to locate the good object and maintain an unmediated and gratifying relationship with it).

It is often held that while Freud had very little by way of infant observation, Winnicott fortified his analytic work with a hefty dose of paediatric training, observation and insight. Except for the *fort-da* and Little Hans, Freud had to reconstruct infantile sexuality from the distorted impressions of the adult neurotics with whom he worked. Winnicott, on the other hand, or so the story goes, spent a great deal of time watching mothers interact with their infants; he, supposedly, went straight to the source. This is the narrative that has inspired and justified much of the infant observation research in the past three decades in North American psychoanalytic circles. Such a narrative is not only inaccurate, it is also disingenuous and by the account of none other than Winnicott himself who asserts that

> it is not from direct observation of infants so much as from the study of transference in the analytic setting that it is possible to gain a clear view

> of what takes place in infancy itself. This work on infantile dependence derives from the study of transference and counter-transference phenomena that belong to the psychoanalyst's involvement with the borderline case. . . . Freud was able to discover infantile sexuality in a new way because he reconstructed it from his analytic work with psycho-neurotic patients. In extending his work to cover the treatment of the borderline psychotic patient it is possible for us to reconstruct the dynamics of infancy and of infantile dependence, and the maternal care that meets this dependence. ('The Theory of the Parent–Infant Relationship', 54–55)

Psychoanalytically, there is nothing exceptional, or even out of the ordinary, to the reconstructive basis of Winnicott's methodology. Built into it, however, is an ideological bias as to the nature of good mothering and, by extension, for Winnicott at least, good psychoanalysing. A good mother is the one who secures for her infant an environment that is protective, holding and providing – empathically rather than mechanistically. She does so without being instructed and while being totally unaware of the theory. In fact, for Winnicott, ignorance is bliss here and practice makes anything but perfect:

> [M]others who have had several children begin to be so good at the technique of mothering that they do all the right things at the right moments, and then the infant who has begun to become separate from the mother has no means of gaining control of all the good things that are going on. . . . In this way the mother, by being a seemingly good mother, does something worse than castrate the infant. The latter is left with two alternatives: either being in a permanent state of regression and of being merged with the mother, or else staging a total rejection of the mother, even of the seemingly good mother. ('The Theory of the Parent–Infant Relationship', 51)

Winnicott's mother must be good 'enough'. She cannot be too good; otherwise she becomes bad. In a very troubling sense, she is trapped in a dilemma: on one hand, she cannot be instructed in the art of good mothering and, indeed, her experience in such matters is potentially a liability rather than an advantage; yet, and on the other hand, her failure at securing the necessary environmental provisions for her child is identified as a significant contributing factor to infantile psychosis or a liability to psychosis at a later date. Winnicott benignly refers to this dilemma in responsibility as 'strange' and his awed followers might see his willingness to identify it in such terms as testimony to his 'paradoxical' thinking. Interestingly enough, this sophistication in insight and judgement was almost entirely lacking when, as head of a 1953 IPA 'mission' to assess the eligibility of Lacan's Société Française de Psychanalyse (SFP) for IPA affiliation – an affiliation that was subsequently denied – Winnicott characterized the work of some of the SFP's most experienced and innovative child psychoanalysts (Françoise Dolto being among the most notable) as 'harmful' since their work supposedly relied on too much intuition and not enough 'method'.[19] Apparently, and while insisting on an intrinsic connection and parallel between the two processes, Winnicott held that though the pursuit of method is harmful for mothering it is most necessary for psychoanalysing. Perhaps that too is . . . 'paradoxical'.

Clinically, a post-Winnicottian generation of psychoanalysts has gathered under the banner of 'Self Psychology' and taken up the motherly function and its attendant lessons of care as a way of marking itself off from the prevailing but presumably highly inefficient Ego Psychological paradigm of indifferent truth and cold knowledge. In the process, this generation has also surrendered its fate to the double bind that is implicit in the Winnicottian 'no one is going to tell you how to do it but you'd better do it right; otherwise. . .' attitude. At its extreme, this double bind is now sadly and unwittingly transformed into a theoretical justification and a privileging of the psychoanalyst who fits the clinical picture that Freud had previously diagnosed as melancholic.[20] Note, in this regard, the Self Psychologist's (1) inability to relinquish the ideal, and hence dead, object (the unmediated and gratifying mother); (2) identification with the dead object (psychoanalyst as substitute, but no less legitimate, source of gratification); (3) and thanks to a most efficient instance of reaction formation, sadism metamorphosed into self-deprecation (readiness to assume responsibility for every disruption in the gratification as index of the psychoanalyst's empathic failure); (4) self-exposure (analysis is the analysis of the counter-transference); and (5) narcissism (cure is tantamount to an internalization of the supposedly healthy psychoanalyst). And the list goes on.

Father

Of course, there is another side to Winnicott, the one that his followers the advocates of caring environments and good enough mothering would all too gladly see ignored. In his elaborations on the counter-transference, Winnicott came to distinguish between three types of responses the psychoanalyst will experience in the face of an analysand's transferential demands and phantasies: (1) a subjective counter-transference stemming from the psychoanalyst's own un-worked through psychology, and hence an obstacle and an interference; (2) a subjective counter-transference rooted in a trait, background or experience shared by both analyst and analysand, and hence a bridge for further empathy and understanding; and, finally (3) an objective counter-transference appropriately experienced by any sufficiently analysed, and hence qualified, psychoanalyst in any given situation. Winnicott understood the last of these responses as a projection of a part of the analysand's own psychology and hence as a useful pointer to the correct therapeutic intervention. In a classic clinical illustration from his 'Hate in the Counter-transference', Winnicott judges as 'objective' his intense negative response to the manoeuvres of an exceptionally troublesome adolescent patient; Winnicott's is the response any other analyst in his position would have felt. Winnicott goes on to deploy that response as sufficient justification for the disciplining action the boy deserves and that the responsible psychoanalyst must be only too happy to deliver: the boy shall be left outside, rain or shine, and not allowed back in till after he'd calmed down. No, Winnicott does not suffer from a Jekyll and Hyde complex. What we have here is merely the other side, the austere and disciplining paternal side of truth, of the same parental coin.

If the maternal metaphor is grounded in a simplistic two-person psychology, the paternal metaphor harks back to and ultimately is hardly anything more than a re-framing of Ego Psychology's atomistic view, presumably the view from which Winnicott had extricated himself. There is barely any structural difference between the model of the psychoanalyst as merely a blank screen onto which pathology gets projected and that of the psychoanalyst as an empty vessel into which pathology gets projected. It is in terms of this dynamic of projection that Winnicott understands the hate he feels toward his adolescent patient; the hate is in fact entirely that patient's; it is engendered by the very things the latter does in his 'crude' way of loving ('Hate in the Counter-transference', 203). The enactment of such a hate by the psychoanalyst is hence justified, for Winnicott at least, on the grounds that the patient can appreciate only what he is capable of feeling (195).[21] Ultimately, Winnicott substitutes the interpretation and resolution of the transference with that of the analysand's hate, via the psychoanalyst's, as the culmination of analytic work prior to which the 'patient is kept to some extent in the position of infant – one who cannot understand what he owes to his mother [or to his psychoanalyst]' (202). Winnicott's message here is twofold: (1) there are times when verbal communication may be legitimately substituted with affective enactment as the preferred mode of analytic work; and (2) the responsibility for such an enactment is solely, and yet again, the analysand's psychology; as for the psychoanalyst, he is merely its 'objective' conduit.

Besides this dynamic of projection, what further reinforces for Winnicott his conviction that hate is at times 'objective', rather than the by-product of an unresolved psychological schema for instance, is a standard associated with the notion of a 'mature healthy adult'. If, at any given moment, the psychoanalyst's affective experience is equivalent to that of what would be expected from said adult, that experience is justifiable and henceforth deemed 'objective'; here, the psychoanalyst is, in a manner of speaking, off the hook.[22] While the masculinist aetiology and cultural baggage of this notion of a 'mature healthy adult' is a justifiable target for a feminist critique,[23] ridding that notion of its male specificity and speaking instead of the mature but genderless healthy adult does not really help matters all that much. In either case, the notion functions as the unacknowledged but self-serving third without which the entire structure would collapse. Winnicott's appeal to the truths and standards of such a 'third' tells the lie to his privileging as evident and self-sufficient the dyadic mother–infant relationship and its attendant gratifications.

Ultimately, Winnicott's 'healthy' adult could only be defined as he, or she, who has been the subject of sound parenting at the hands of a 'good enough' parent and/or a psychoanalyst as parent. Structurally, the bottom line is that such an adult is deployed to justify and legitimize a process of which he or she is also the product. Instead of recognizing the self-serving circularity of the argument, it is the recipient and provider of good parenting who emerges into the mind of the psychoanalyst as the standard of health and of appropriate clinical practice. If, as Freud had insisted, fetishism befalls he who disavows the reality of the vagina in order to safeguard his penis, then equally liable to that condition is the psychoanalyst who disavows the circularity of the Winnicottian approach for fear of losing his only pole of health.

Child

It might be convenient here to argue for a Winnicottian distinction in clinical matters, a distinction between motherly comfort and fatherly rigour, a distinction that would allow Winnicott's follower, at any given clinical moment, to pick and choose of the text or the practice whichever of the two positions is useful and/or appropriate. Let me at this point highlight yet another of Winnicott's significant 'paradoxes', one that undermines both options. The 'paradox' in question is formulated in terms of an implicit expectation that the psychoanalyst occupy the position of parent and the analysand that of child in the context of a therapy initially pursued precisely because said analysand is suffering from being much too encumbered by the demands and strictures of the external world, much too preoccupied with the responsibilities of productivity and efficiency and much too burdened under the weight of a rigid and stagnant life. If, and mine is a highly tentative and conditional 'if', the parental metaphor is to have any relevance at all in psychoanalytic practice, then it seems to me that it would be more consistent and indeed useful to argue that it is precisely the psychoanalyst who occupies the role of the curious and, dare I say it, 'passionate' child who is always on the lookout for opportunities to elicit more playful stories, fantasies and associations from an 'adult' analysand who wants nothing more than to resolve life's dilemmas as concretely and expediently, which is to say as un-psychoanalytically, as possible.[24]

Reproduction

To return to the suggested choice between truthful father and caring mother, I think it would be more accurate, interesting and even fruitful to argue for a structural link and perhaps even a necessary implication between these two positions, and hence between melancholia and fetishism as their underlying modes of operation. The argument would highlight the fetishistic pleasure in melancholia and the melancholic repetition in fetishism, both theoretically and clinically. It would uncover the melancholic psychoanalyst's disavowal of the inevitably frustrating mother and the fetishistic psychoanalyst's repetitively self-tormenting pursuit of a sphere free from the much-dreaded subjective counter-transference. I shall have to leave this argument for another place and another time. For now, what I would like to underscore is that, in matters clinical, the parental metaphor retains its full force not only as the guide for sound clinical practice but also as the desirable therapeutic outcome.

The internalization of the caring mother and the identification with the equitable father are not ends in themselves; they are the stages that must pave the way for motherhood and/or fatherhood as the primary goals of the therapeutic process. Ultimately, what we have here is not only a vision of psychoanalysis as a parenting practice but of parenting as the mark of analytic health. If the psychoanalyst as parent were the paragon of said health, then it would stand to reason that he or she would only wish the best of health for his or her analysand as offspring, as any 'good enough' parent would. It must then stand to reason that the psychoanalyst as such a parent would wish the analysand to become a parent in turn. Parenting implies a reproduction where supposedly love and work meet to reach their highest potential. At this point, the objection may be raised that perhaps it is Eriksonian generativity that lies at the heart of the analytic understanding of health and that biological reproduction may be its most obvious but not necessarily only expression. While that may very well be the case, the fact remains that it is non-reproductive sexuality, with all its variations on the themes of inversion and perversion, rather than a poor or non-existent 'generativity' that has been pathologized by much of psychoanalysis.

The flip side of a categorical imperative is a taboo. The flip side of an injunction to move in a specific direction is the injunction to restrain oneself against the lure and temptations of its opposite. If reproduction is a necessary component of that which psychoanalysis has come to hold as the epitome of health, non-reproduction, or those components of sexuality that are assumed to be tantamount to non-reproduction, become at best obstacles to be surmounted and at worst taboos to be avoided at all costs.[25] For the most part, the psychoanalytic profession has picked up this bias and translated it into the covert but compelling ground for a methodology and a morality that are mutually justifying. Though for very different clinical, theoretical and cultural reasons, the exceptions to this rule (branches of Lacanian and relational analysis) stand out in their opposition to the parental metaphor as both clinical standard and therapeutic outcome. It is not a coincidence that both groups do not belong to the IPA, and that both groups have not considered, and as a matter of principle, homosexuality as the other dark continent of psychoanalysis, or that analysands open about their non-reproductive same-sex proclivities as undesirable social deviants. Indeed, and long before the rise of the cultural demand for tolerance and diversity, Lacan was among the earliest of analysts to welcome such individuals into his practice without feeling the need to redress or cure their homoerotic desires.[26] Moreover, it was Lacan's refusal to abide by the IPA's standard of judging inversion as sufficient grounds for disqualification from the ranks of the profession that was as instrumental in his own subsequent barring from membership in the Association as was his questionable practice of the so-called 'variable-length' session.

For all his shortcomings, and in highlighting the constitutive function of hate in the counter-transference, Winnicott points not only to the psychoanalyst's inherently ambivalent stance vis-à-vis the analysand but also, inadvertently and perhaps even unwittingly, to that of the parent toward the child. André Green is yet another major analytic theorist who has pursued a similar line of thought in suggesting that the Oedipal wish to kill the father need not be all that shocking or incomprehensible when the father himself had already experienced the son as a rival and acted on the wish to get rid of him.[27] Winnicott and Green point not so much to a parenting that is failed, perverted or derailed. Their observations strike at the core of our stock of platitudes that collapse the 'healthy' onto the 'loving' when it comes to parenting and psychoanalysing. What is striking here is the resilience and longevity of such insipid and one-dimensional notions of relating in the context of a therapeutic culture that, for the most part, has recognized ambivalence as a central psychological dynamic. Indeed, and before both Winnicott and Green, Freud had already uncovered underneath the supposedly secure and balanced growth of the child an inevitable struggle through often confusing but invariably highly tumultuous series of psychological challenges and dilemmas. Likewise, and rather than succumbing to the clichés and romanticizations of childhood 'innocence', Klein too had helped uncover the infant's aggressions, depressions and paranoias.

Work

Freud grounded psychoanalysis in terms of a collaborative uncovering of the unconscious as dynamic and overdetermined. That such uncovering occurs in a fraction of the time 'psychoanalysis' occupies or that it necessitates much preparation does not deny it its status as the core and defining element of the practice; if anything, it reinforces it as the however infinitesimally small but not any the less defining marker of a practice that is singular and specific, a practice that is irreducible to this or that of the modes of relating with which we are already familiar. That such uncovering leaves open the questions of 'efficacy' and so-called 'therapeutic value' that, in other words, the uncovering does not necessarily make people 'feel better', assuming we already know and agree on what the expression actually means, the way doctors and parents are presumably supposed to make patients and children 'feel better', may be a concern for those attempting to justify the practice in the eyes of a culture grounded in the principles of expediency and comfort. But it is precisely the work of such a culture that psychoanalysis has been designed to counter. This is no less true nowadays than it was in the time of Freud. Sadly, the practice has become increasingly consolidated around the safety and satisfaction certain objects may bring to the process of reproduction and less around the complexity and unpredictability of our desires.

It is for this reason that, I believe, the parental metaphor has continued to hold such a sway over the profession. Unlike all the other models that have enjoyed varying degrees of success (I am thinking of friendship, education, witnessing or even healing) parenting comes closest to elevating repetition from a basic physiological event and/or a pathological compulsion to the status of a stable and overarching principle of psychic life. However, and by the standards of not only this or that of the various leading orientations in psychoanalytic theory or practice but by those standards that the discipline itself has held as its foundational and distinguishing mark, repetition could not be any further from either the truth of the unconscious or, for that matter, the history of its science. As regards the former, and even at those times when the unconscious is trapped in the most monotonous and debilitating of cyclical scenarios, it is still, and however minimally, an unconscious that dreams, phantasises, mourns, defers, displaces, remembers, thinks and compromises; it is still an unconscious that works. It is a machine, as Deleuze and Guattari will put it, that affords a rest only once in its lifetime, in that very same ground where it finds its final resting place. Otherwise, it is in constant movement. As for the science of the unconscious, it has managed to thrive precisely because many of its practitioners, famous or otherwise, have resisted the institutional demands and methodological requirements for repetition and homogeneity.

Chapter Three

Anti-Oedipus: reading, listening, analysing

'It is at work everywhere, at times continually, at others intermittently. It breathes, it heats, it eats. It shits, it fucks' (*AO*, F7, E1).[28] These could hardly qualify as the opening words of a scientific treatise on the workings of the psyche; they read even less as the words that would announce a measured and respectful adherence to the philosophical rules of engagement. With their staccato tone[29] and visceral, if not at times crude, content, these words demand attention; they interrupt; they intervene. And yet, they do not come from an obviously rebellious outside to either psychoanalysis or philosophy. Indeed, at the time they were published, their authors could not have been any closer to the centres of two of the most vibrant intellectual spheres in the Paris of the early 1970s.

First, there is Gilles Deleuze, the university professor who had already made his mark on the academic scene with a series of ground-breaking monographs on Hume, Proust, Spinoza, Kant, von Sacher-Masoch, Bergson and, last but not least, Nietzsche. Much like his fellow attendees of Jacques Lacan's seminar, Deleuze was heavily invested in revitalizing psychoanalytic theory and rescuing it from its bureaucratic and assimilationist doldrums. He had already deemed Freud's 'Beyond the Pleasure Principle' a 'masterpiece' whose author had engaged penetratingly in philosophical reflection (*Coldness and Cruelty*, 111) and much of his *Difference and Repetition* was an engagement with the classic psychoanalytic notions referenced in the monograph's title. Along with *The Logic of Sense*, *Difference and Repetition* helped confirm Deleuze as not only an insightful historian of ideas but as a member of the newly minted generation of original thinkers poised to lead the intellectual scene, in both France and abroad, for the coming decades.

Felix Guattari, however, had just finished his analysis with Lacan and was in private practice as a psychoanalyst and member of the *École Freudienne de Paris*. Unlike his collaborator though, Guattari had devoted most of his energies to clinical practices and participatory politics than to writing. By the end of 1972, the year in which *Anti-Oedipus* had made its appearance, only one collection of essays was to bear his signature: *Psychanalyse et transversalité*.[30] In it, and based on his work with Jean Oury at the La Borde clinic[31] during almost two decades, Guattari presented a carefully thought out psychotherapeutic style that is acutely disruptive of its institutional limits.

Both Deleuze and Guattari enjoyed a certain standing, if not cachet, among their peers. Each was well established in his field and neither would have been easily fooled by the lure of a rebellious adolescence. How then is one to explain the forceful and less than 'expert' tone of the opening lines of their work and how is one to salvage their project from the dismissals,[32] the psychologisms,[33] and even, ironically, the censorial adulations[34] that have dominated much of what has already been said or written about the text? The answer that I would like to present in this chapter and begin arguing for is that, rather than simply idiosyncratic or illustrative,[35] the style of *Anti-Oedipus* is inextricably tied to the theory it advocates, that, in other words, the '*Anti-Oedipus*' effect is much less one of shock or affront, promotion or exposition, but of that moment at which the distinctions between style and content, theory and practice, observer and observed cease to hold. I would like to read the assertion 'It is at work everywhere . . .' and all that follows it as belonging to the unconscious as much as it is about that unconscious and hence as telling of that 'irreversible approbation', as Derrida observed of psychoanalysis 30 years later (*De quoi demain*, 271), at the heart of experience and thought, no matter their location, quality, or scale.

Reading

To assert that Deleuze and Guattari's *Anti-Oedipus* not only does not preclude but, in fact, also enacts a psychoanalytic practice demands that one negotiate a certain awkwardness in the face of that history of ideas often hijacked by the priests of continuity, progress, breaks or reversals. The assertion's more serious challenge lies with a by now current 'schizoanalytic' tendency to disinvest the text from any Freudian trace.[36] Deleuze and Guattari's emphatic declaration that 'the schizoanalyst is not an interpreter' (*AO*, F404, E338), reconfirmed a few years later by Deleuze in his dialogues with Claire Parnet under the banner of a 'there is nothing to interpret' (*Dialogues*, 4), is itself an interpretation and would suggest that the 'analysis' in 'schizoanalysis' is nothing but the overlooked residue of a long exhausted attachment or a leftover rotting in a shadowy corner and hence an embarrassment of sorts. Would that such a leftover be the slip conveniently interpreted in light of the very theory it jettisons. Suffice it to say at this point that the substitution of 'psycho' with 'schizo' is not without its own difficulties.

In due course, we shall have to identify some of these difficulties in terms of, among others, the inherently libratory potential attributed to the schizophrenic process[37] as necessarily contaminated by its dangerous proximity to, and even dependence on, the motif and spirit of purity. For now, we have to ask as to why this leftover, this 'analysis', was not consumed at the bacchanalian feast or dispensed with immediately afterwards. Presumably, one is to expect nothing less from the advocates and practitioners of 'extraordinary words' as Deleuze would put it (*Dialogues*, 3) – unless, that is, a hint is being given, or better still, a hint is to be made.

We are hence confronted from the very start with the question of interpretation: if, indeed, there is nothing to interpret, nothing to uncover, then what is it that we are doing or that we can do while remaining connected to the relay that is the text? For those of us familiar with the rhetoric surrounding Deleuze and Guattari, the answer is quite familiar: the text is but a toolbox; it offers itself as an opening onto new spaces of action, of thought, of thought as action.[38] However, and though we have supposedly learned our lessons well, we repeatedly find ourselves under the sway of one of two radically opposed tendencies. The first is to trace theoretical genealogies that trap the text in the shadows of such figures as Marx and Freud genealogies that highlight the ingenuity of the text's authors and, in so doing, subordinate the entire schema of texts, authors and readers to the hierarchy that we have come to recognize as the History of Ideas. The second tendency veers in an anti-theoretical direction, fiercely denouncing the so-called earnestness of any attempt at understanding as ostensibly castrating since to understand is to supposedly excise the radical impetus, the laughter and the momentum they generate.

The former tendency forces the text into that sphere of the public domain that is subjugated to the standards of clarity and authority. With such standards in hand, the text is rendered as a Nietzschean reordering of Marx and Freud. No: perhaps it is Nietzschean redemption of a Marxism polluted, crippled even, by the degeneration of the time's Sino-Soviet socialism, a redemption that has abandoned any allegiance to the dominant Freudianism of the day. No, no, no: the text is actually an implicit engagement with and a repudiation of Lacan through Freud; after all, it is a radical materialist psychiatry that remains the central concern here. The theories, and the interpretations, abound as they jostle for first place in that academic pantheon appropriately known as secondary literature. Meanwhile, the latter tendency has forced the text into a private domain of so-called nomadic manipulations and appropriations, a domain where communication and collaboration are, unfortunately, rendered quasi-impossible.

One is stuck between, on the one hand, the 'royal' Law that dictates how the text ought to be read and where best it might be placed in the Grand History of Thought and, on the other, the threat of a dis-integration into the realm of a crippled and crippling atomism. It would be convenient at this point to map such tendencies onto the very processes that Deleuze and Guattari have diagnosed in other writings, especially in *Kafka: Toward a Minor Literature* and *A Thousand Plateaus*, and to argue that, for instance, the tension one experiences is none other than the one operating between the two limits of the royally totalizing and the nomadically dispersive, the very same tension through which history is said to unfold and action to emerge. Though this strategy may prove to be quite fruitful, it cannot overcome its basic flaw of reducing our responses to the text, and in the process the text itself, to the status of yet another example of those dualities that have suffused the authors' work: active/reactive, molecular/molar, minor/major. The flaw resides in the strategy's progressivist revisionism, in what Guattari would criticise later as a 'dominant grammaticality' ('Semiological Subjection', 143) according to which the various parts are subordinated to the logic of the whole, its essence and final outcome – be it meaning cure, or profit.

One of the strategies I want to adopt in this and the following chapters is based in the principle of simultaneity, of the simultaneity of past and present, of thought and action, of understanding and affect, of clinic and academy. This strategy is in line with a concern that is pragmatic, which is not to say non- or anti-theoretical. As Foucault had indicated in his introduction to the English translation of the work,[39] as Deleuze had reiterated in 'Intellectuals and Power',[40] and as Guattari had stressed on many occasions, the text demonstrates not the transmission of information but the communication of a conflictual and undomesticated desire through what Guattari describes as a 'richly expressive situation in which a whole series of semiotic components are involved' ('Desire is Power', 16).

The desire that is mine in this context is, among other things, a desire to listen, to read, to think and, indeed, to analyse. In response to the crypto-Deleuzo-Guattarians' declaration (or, more accurately, expression of a wish) that *Anti-Oedipus* functions as the Medusa into whose face psychoanalysis, and Freud in particular, cannot but stare and subsequently suffer the most definitive, if not abominable, of deaths, I want to insist on the text's inherently analytic dimension. To do otherwise would be to wrest it from its theoretical and practical matrix and reduce to the banal, to reify, its authors' richly ambivalent response to a tradition in which they rarely ceased to participate theoretically and, in the case of Guattari, clinically.[41] Guattari's own appraisal of the situation from a lecture he wrote in 1977 and delivered in Mexico in 1981, and hence after his and Deleuze's presumed departure from anything psychoanalytic,[42] hardly needs any elaboration:

> After years of training and practice I have come to the conclusion that if psychoanalysis does not radically reform its methods and its theoretical references it will lose all credibility, *which I would find regrettable on several counts.* In fact, it would hardly matter to me if psychoanalytic societies, schools, or even the profession itself were to disappear, *so long as the analysis of the unconscious reaffirms its legitimacy and renews its theoretical and practical modalities.* ('Beyond the Psychoanalytical Unconscious', 193, emphasis added)[43]

Ultimately, the Freudian presence in the anti-oedipal project cannot be subsumed in its entirety under the register of neurotic stasis. Alongside Deleuze and Guattari's mostly justifiable critique of the cynically essentialist and normalizing vein in the history of psychoanalysis, there also lies their tremendously active and creatively fetishistic disavowal of some of the principal elements of Freudian thought, a disavowal that invites, even begs, to be distorted, reproduced and ultimately disavowed. Deleuze himself had praised such a disavowal as 'nothing less than the foundation of imagination' (*Coldness and Cruelty*, 128) and, along with Guattari, had gone on to trace its passages and vicissitudes via Levi-Strauss' concept of *bricolage*, culminating with the anti-oedipal rubric of desiring production. To put it in the language of the text, if the flow from, among others, the desiring-machine 'Freud' has been interrupted, consumed, or drawn off by that other machine 'Deleuze-Guattari' with the first volume of *Capitalism and Schizophrenia* for an outcome, the reversal, doubling and furthering of such a flow may be, if not equally inspiring, at least productive, even if minimally. It is with this productivity in mind that I read the text; I do so not for the sake of a *rapprochement* between Freud and Deleuze and Guattari; I am even less interested in settling the question as to which of the two versions of analysis is the more accurate, justifiable or liberating. At issue for me here is analysis per se, as a practice and a process.

Writing

Of his role as historian of ideas, Deleuze once wrote of a capacity to produce the monstrous 'other' through the act of writing, analysing, and schizoanalysing ('Lettre à un critique sévère', 15). *Anti-Oedipus* stands apart in tone and intensity from all that Deleuze and Guattari have written, separately and together. They themselves are made other in that work.[44] Guattari would contribute such notions as desiring-machines, transversality and subject-groups to the collaborative work but would experience most of his other major anchors and references demolished in the process – Lacan and Mao most notably ('Everywhere at Once', 30). Deleuze would bring a certain theoretical rigour to bear on the material at hand but would also be overcome with a febrile and decidedly un-'philosophical' tone in his seminars at the time at Vincennes.[45]

Knowing this about the authors' backgrounds prior to *Anti-Oedipus* and the effects the project had on them once it was accomplished sheds light not so much on the sources and patterns of the text's principal themes but on the fact that the project was inherently disruptive, transforming and productive of the different as monstrous and hence unrecognizable. This is one of the distinguishing features not only of the text but also of what it advocates. Indeed, and in one of its principal tasks, schizoanalysis is a fundamentally unruly process that pays little attention to law or history as fixed cause, genetic explanation or testimony to developmental conflicts or deficits. There is much too much that is happening for it to be subsumed under any one category or set of categories. There is much too much that is at work for it to be a meaning, a motivation, or, ostensibly, a truth that lies at the core of one's being, a truth with which one is to consciously align. Invariably, there is much too much possibility for there to be only one future (integration, genital love or the depressive position) the analysand would have otherwise had but for the traumata.

In another respect, Deleuze and Guattari's antagonistic attitude toward all that is hierarchical in psychoanalysis (the institution, the theory and the practice) offers only a partial explanation as to why the highly regimented and at times virulently anti-intellectual community of clinicians has dismissed *Anti-Oedipus* as at best irrelevant and at worst irresponsible. Most problematic for that community has been Deleuze and Guattari's trespassing of the clinical and theoretical limits of an unconscious whose dynamics have been stripped of any considerations beyond those of an objective, universal and stratified syntax. Indeed, Freud's successors have generally repudiated any deviation from their generalized analytic norm as, at best, a confused and confusing theoretical error or a metaphysical construct substantiated by neither association nor affect. Such a resistance is hardly surprising for one need only remind oneself of quasi-existential concerns around legitimacy, territoriality and credibility to which the psychoanalytic community has never been immune. In the present context, this resistance is not entirely unwarranted since the encounter before us does not involve an amicable or liberal exchange but a serious questioning, and hence rewriting, of both therapy and theory.

For Deleuze and Guattari, the unconscious is machinic; it is productive rather than representational; it is culturally and historically permeable; its diverse and conflictual investments include the bodily, linguistic, ethological and economic. For Deleuze and Guattari, the problem facing psychoanalysis lies in its failure to recognize the instability and mutability of its point of concern (the unconscious) and, by extension, to recognize the historicity of its own standards and principles. More specifically, the anti-oedipal critique of psychoanalysis unfolds along three intersecting planes:

1. The theory is a representational model that binds the unconscious to repetition and lack.
2. The clinical practice is a self-serving interpretation that produces a docile and assimilated subject.
3. The institution is a stagnant hierarchy that breeds divisiveness and scapegoating.

This is particularly evident in the context of a discipline whose intellectual roots have been nourished by the late nineteenth century's rejection of the Enlightenment view of the human psyche as self-evident, rational and autonomous. Ironically, and through a momentous transformation of modernity's 'it is' into a therapeutic 'it shall be', the analytic movement has for the most part tried to rewrite its own history and to incorporate itself into the very tradition it had initially set out to question. In so doing, it has pursued not only its acceptance into the cultural and scientific fold but also its ascension to the status of a meta-discourse guiding, profiting from and hence inevitably defending society's various centres of power. Unfortunately, it is not so much in spite of but rather because of its anxious pursuit of medico-scientific legitimacy that, for instance, the North American variant of psychoanalysis is currently marginalized. The practice has failed to respond to the singularities and transformations in psychic life that cannot be subsumed under any generalized categories, be they of castration, signification or subjectivity. All such categories point to the endorsement of the principle of a normalized reproduction and integration as the single most important marker of mental health. It is hence hardly a surprise, but not any the less perplexing and indeed troubling, that, though a quintessentially urban practice, psychoanalysis has for the most part remained glued to a caricature version of the suburban as the highest accomplishment in psychic life.

It is crucial to note at this point that, though they call for a redeployment of the anti-modernist impetus in psychoanalysis, Deleuze and Guattari are far from aligning themselves with the vulgates of the post-modern. The master discourse has not died and the fragmentation of identity is hardly a recent occurrence. Both phenomena have persisted, and will continue to persist throughout the course of human history – unless, that is, the perpetual rearrangement of subjectivity, its productions, and investments is intensified through the analytic project. The requirement here is that the project's tools help one

> understand all the garbage one encounters, not only in one's personal life, but also in institutions and groupuscules, that is to say in all kinds of power relations. And conversely [adds Guattari] . . . if you are not capable of understanding someone's difficulties in light of the social investments and collective subjectivity involved, none of it can work. ('So What', 9)

This understanding is not the effect of merely acquainting oneself with the economic and/or cultural specificities of one's analysands for instance. Nor is it the outcome of an eclectic, multidisciplinary stance that allows one a more integrated and deeper knowledge of the subject the higher the pile of perspectives one accrues. Among the contributions to the schizoanalytic project that can be attributed directly to Guattari, and there are many, is the practice of transversality, of lateral intra-disciplinary moves that consist in extracting elements and procedures from one domain and transferring them onto other heterogeneous fields of inquiry ('I Am an Idea Thief', 40).[46] The results are unpredictable and may indeed turn out to be utterly useless. Still, one needs to allow and recognize for oneself a measure of failure. When schizoanalytic, psychoanalysis is no longer a codified practice, a closed set of rules that stem from and subsequently govern the private exchange between two individuals; nor is it a discourse that informs but remains impermeable to extra-clinical phenomena, as the rubric of 'applied' psychoanalysis continues to be conceived and practiced. Rather, psychoanalysis becomes one of a multitude of concrete machines capable of traversing various scales of reference, creating singularities and, in the process, undergoing their own singularization.

Ultimately, I would like to argue that, as much as it may be the harshest and most insightful critique of psychoanalysis we have to date, *Anti-Oedipus* is more radically a practice of transversality, a reworking of basic analytic principles and strategies in accordance with the dynamics attributed to the unconscious as a form of thought, and hence as a process rather than a locality. Put differently, *Anti-Oedipus* is the becoming-unconscious, the becoming-unconscious-as-machine of psychoanalysis. Undoubtedly, some clinicians will be made most uncomfortable by this declaration. Theirs has been the task of going into the cage in order to tame the beast (psychoanalysis), to make it more scientific, curative, reproductive. On the opposite side of the divide, many Deleuzo-Guattarians may very well consider my position a betrayal of the most sacrosanct of the masters' intentions – presumably, to cage the beast in order to kill it. Ironically, or maybe not, it is a reversal of roles that we often witness nowadays. Many Deleuzo-Guattarians have tamed the beast (schizoanalysis) by reducing it to the level of a normative and monotonous discourse replete with its own set of prescriptions and denunciations. As for the clinicians, they have either committed themselves to a will to ignorance or simply pretended that the beast, a flash in the pan, is already dead. Needless to say, and fortunately, there are a thousand exceptions to every rule.

Listening

Unlike most texts in the field, *Anti-Oedipus* aims at collapsing the distance and distinction between psychoanalysis and the unconscious, at transforming the one by investing it with the qualities and dynamics it uncovers in the other. The science of the unconscious must henceforth obey the laws of its own object. The becoming-unconscious of psychoanalysis therefore signals neither its death nor its repression but the transformation of its forms of thought into those of its most loved and hated other. Deleuze and Guattari will capitalize on the ambivalence (and how could it be anything but?) that psychoanalysis has had to the unconscious; in the process, they will distinguish themselves from, on the one hand, Ego-Psychology's hatred of its object as it pursues its discipline through the regiments of development and adaptation and, on the other hand, the Lacanian idolization of that selfsame object as the unmoved mover once its registers have presumably settled into their most appropriate of configurations.

In the meantime, and as I have already stated, *Anti-Oedipus* is the becoming-unconscious-as-machine of psychoanalysis. As such, it itself is a machine; as such, it has no meaning; it does not refer to a fixed external reference from which it derives its energy and value. What it does refer to is the unlimited and hence unforeseeable set of effects, machinic in turn, that it may generate. As with any such project, the obstacles and pitfalls we will face are inevitable and numerous. They are reflections of the shifts, movements and breakdowns of the text itself, of the unconscious itself. My concern is then with the effects made available through the text, with what it is capable of doing, as much as with what it means or with the theory it advances. This strategy will help me circumvent the by now stale and stultifying debate in some psychoanalytic circles regarding the status of theory and its relationship to analytic data. Indeed, and for the longest time, a divide has operated between the so-called empiricists, those that challenge the primacy of theory on the grounds that it disturbs and distorts analytic material, and the meta-psychologists, those that insist that without any theory such a material could not be recognized, let alone organized and understood. To avoid the coarseness and disintegration of the former while resisting the totalization of the latter requires that we read, or listen, not so much with a certain degree of patience, awaiting the moment when everything shall be revealed and made to cohere, but with an openness to the surprise,[47] to the interruption and to the shift, to what they may produce and to what they may be made to produce.

Though for the most part exegetical, the strategy that I would like to adopt is also that of a process reading, as in analytic process, of reporting the notes and associations of a listening, my listening, with the third ear or with an evenly suspended attention as some of us clinicians are fond of saying, to the book's opening pages on the three fundamental syntheses of desire. Hopefully, these notes will be read in tandem with the text – rather than instead of the text – and will hence provide a space and an in-between for the reader to produce further notes and associations. At its most superficial level, this strategy is indeed part of a generalized and principled commitment to Guattarian transversality; it should not therefore sound all that foreign to schizoanalytic ears. More importantly however, and while keeping in mind the stakes and limits of such a move, I will attempt to engage the text on its own terms and by the very standards it advances and enacts. I will not go looking for the authors' idiosyncratic but presumably unconscious motivations as they are rendered manifest through the text. Nor will I search for the symbolic 'it' with which Lacan had been so preoccupied. Maelzel's chess-player has been retired sadly and it is not so much the man inside the machine that is my concern but the man or, more appropriately in this case the text, as a machine that is my focus, not in what its authors intended it to say or do but in what it may enable its readers to say or do.

At this point, the concern may be raised that my focus on the introductory and briefest of the sections of *Anti-Oedipus* is much too narrow for an adequate account of a project that has spanned two exceptionally fertile intellectual careers, that, effectively, I have selected my material a bit too conveniently or perhaps even self-servingly. I have two disclaimers in response to this concern. First, I am not interested in articulating a systematic and all-encompassing Deleuze-Guattarian theory of the psyche or in setting the foundations for a new therapeutic practice derived from such a theory. Rather, I would like to concentrate on one moment in Deleuze and Guattari's itinerary, as one would on a vignette, in order to follow its movement as it articulates and enacts its strategies; it is hence in its dynamics that I am most invested. Second, and in the spirit of such an investment, I will not propose a final or exhaustive interpretation of the moment's meaning or intention; I am much more interested in deploying it as a tool and a relay back to psychoanalysis in order to both underscore the richness of its method and, more importantly, trace that method's reflexive effects on its principles and strategies. I am convinced that once psychoanalytic theory and practice meet, once the theory is practiced on itself and finds itself on the couch it has produced, associating, fantasizing, slipping, it discovers itself anew, in a most singular and desiring position.

Finally, a minor detour and a comment regarding the published English translation, its inaccuracies, inconsistencies and its heaviness even are in order. Some would hold up the flow of the French original as a sad and perhaps irrecoverable loss for the reader of its English rendering. In one respect, I am quite sympathetic to that position and shall, whenever relevant, point to the losses and attempt to bridge the gaps. Interestingly, this situation runs parallel to the clinical concern regarding the original 'mother' tongue, a concern that the literature has often debated.[48] What are the effects, losses and/or by-products of an analytic process taken up in a language other than that through which one's earliest experiences were registered and processed? If one were to pursue the most crucial of connections between affect and word for instance, how could such an analysis but be incomplete? Contra this logic of purity, I would like to suggest that, often enough, it is precisely in the process of accounting to an other in a language that is not one's own and through the derailings and breakdowns of such a process that one can begin to understand one's history without the risk of collusion or oversimplification. Indeed, and if, among other things, psychoanalysis is that process through which one begins to speak, learn and understand the language of one's own other, of one's unconscious, then one need not fear to stutter, to question, to rethink and to rewrite.

Analysing

It is typical for an analytic treatment to begin with a series of fact-gathering consultations or 'interviews' during which the analyst enquires as to the prospective analysand's history and dynamics. In taking a history, the analyst is on the lookout for patterns of conflict, relatedness, identification, defence, affect, loss or cohesion. Depending on school or orientation, this initial stage may last anywhere from one session to one year. Regardless of school or orientation, a diagnostic hypothesis is being formulated, even if implicitly.[49] Of course, the scales of reference may vary widely, as indeed they often do, and, eventually, the analyst's hypotheses may very well be fine-tuned or altogether reframed as the work progresses. The purpose of such a procedure is to inform the analyst of the analysand's psychological terrain so as to better gear the tone and focus of the interventions. Something very similar often takes place in the initial stages of an encounter with a text: the reader mines the flow of content and method for pointers and motifs that will open onto the world that is being conveyed.

Now imagine if you will a prospective analysand who, in an initial consultation, rushes through a chaotic, directionless and conflictual presentation. The first hints of insanity are already with us. Analysts from various schools may disagree vastly on the symptomatology. For some, it might be the neologisms or words that are quite ordinary but whose arrangements are neither predictable nor intelligible (desiring-production, body-without-organs, celibate and miraculating machines). For others, it might be the absurd insistence on a total breakdown of the boundaries between self and other, inside and outside. For others still, it might be the ego-syntonic disregard for the fundamental rule of communication, the identification-provenance rule: this is who I am and this is where I come from. The diagnosis, however, will rarely differ. What we have here is clear and incontrovertible evidence of a borderline if not indeed psychotic organization; this person is quite likely un-analysable. The reader will have already formed a parallel opinion: the language is crude (fuck, shit, arse); the concepts make no sense (machines that work only when they breakdown); the overall strategy is dismissive of a long history of authoritative research and scholarship (after all, fiction writers and madmen hardly qualify as expert sources in the field – no?); and, last but not least, the tone of the text is highly polemical thus disqualifying it from rigorous theoretical merit, and yet its content is devoid of any concrete plans and strategies as to how to fight the oppressor thus rendering it utterly irrelevant to the frontline activist. This text is almost certainly unreadable.

'Given a certain effect, what machine could produce it?' (*AO*, F8, E3). In the first instance, we have the answers that Deleuze and Guattari have explored in interviews published following the appearance of *Anti-Oedipus*. Attempting the connections between the text and these interviews meets with the obstacle that is the fundamental distinction at the heart of the analytic procedure, the distinction between the often nuanced and dimmed voice of the unconscious as the most authentic representative of the psyche, and the derivative, defensive and distorting noises of the everyday. The not entirely unreasonable objection might be raised that, in taking stock of the interviews and their answers, we have departed from the text and hence from the material that ought to be our sole concern. In effect, we have broken the analytic frame by seeking the assistance of other informants who, though they may carry the identificatory markers 'Deleuze' and 'Guattari', are not the same as those that produced the text and lived it. Presumably, we have forsaken the rich experience of free associations in favour of a distanced and organized secondary revision.

For psychoanalysis, though key, the distinction between the conscious and the unconscious is not universal; it applies primarily to the neurotic. The problem of psychosis, and schizophrenia in particular, is precisely that such a distinction or separation has not been fully erected; Oedipus, the father function, the Law, has not been installed properly and the individual is left under the sway of the double-headed monster incest-murder. The clinical insistence on the frame (frequency and length of sessions, payment schedules, breaks, extra-sessional communications) parallels this distinction and is designed initially to strengthen it, to contain and boost ego-functions in order to facilitate the subsequent exploration and articulation of that monster's logic. Unless analysed, a break in the frame may tamper with the often-delicate balance of the psychic apparatus. The text's opening words 'It is at work everywhere' are an unmitigated rejection of this claustrophobic distinction. The implication here is that the delicate balance that psychoanalysis attempts to maintain is actually the one it seeks to establish or consolidate. It (the unconscious, the id) is not lodged or hidden away in the darkest recesses of our minds. It is everywhere. It is not a repository of word or thing presentations. It is at work everywhere. Repression is not the holding back of content or affect; it is rather a blockage of work, of production. Cast in the language of Deleuze's *Nietzsche and Philosophy* from the early 1960s, repression is reactive and the reactive is that category of forces that prevent other forces from doing what they can. For this to actually happen between any two given forces, both must operate on the same surface. Psychological depth becomes the effect that is produced by the psychoanalytic machine. It is not on the basis of its supposed inaccuracy that Deleuze and Guattari will reject it but rather because of the unwarranted effects of discipline and privilege it will in turn generate.

Take the dream for instance. Freud first unravelled its tripartite structure in terms of an unconscious latent thought (a primary wish), a distorting process of dream work (condensation and displacement being its two most effective components) and a manifest content (the often disjointed and nonsensical visual imagery that we identify as 'the dream'). Much of the dream interpreter's initial efforts were suffused with the intrigue and power, often military, at the heart of a classically cryptographic paradigm: a plaintext scrambled into a cyphertext by means of an algorithm of substitution and transposition. Interestingly enough, the interpreter and code breaker's focus will shift over the years from primary wish to dream work, from plaintext to algorithm, and hence from meaning to thought process as the most significant component of the apparatus.[50] Nevertheless, Freud will persist in thinking the unconscious, in terms of both content and process, as deep, hidden and covered over. A Heideggerian before Heidegger, he will identify the covering over as the falsehood psychoanalysis is designed to redress – after its own fashion, of course.

Let us not fall into the trap of attributing to *Anti-Oedipus* the effect of collapsing the entirety of the depth that is the topographical model onto a single plane. Such a collapse carries a descriptive authority and an accuracy in terms of its rendering of the psyche that the text is least interested in. Deleuze and Guattari's question is 'what machine is capable of producing a certain effect?' and not 'on what plane is a machine situated with respect to its effect?' The full sweep with which the text opens, 'it is at work everywhere', marks no distinction between depth and surface, conscious and unconscious, truth and error. Not even the distinction between machine and effect is upheld since the one is invariably also the other for another. What we are facing is not so much the terrain's collapse or expansion to the nth degree, but rather its dis-organization. This is no mere quibble over the number of dimensions that will best approximate the reality of the psyche: two, or three or a thousand. This is an outright rejection of the very attempt to delineate, to quantify and to fix the components along any structural lines – topographic, linguistic or affective. The cartography for which Guattari has become famous is one in which the elements are in constant movement; it is a cartography that lays no claim to topological accuracy; it is not intended to get someone somewhere but to get someone moving, drifting even. The echoes of the psycho-geography of the Situationist International are fairly distinct here.[51] But so are the echoes of psychoanalysis as an adventure unprejudiced in terms of its aims and modalities.

Producing

Let us follow these echoes then, if only temporarily, to appreciate what else we are being offered, both within the text and in those expressions that have preceded or come to succeed it. Let us go back to the histories and interviews, to the processes and machines that are identified as the producers of *Anti-Oedipus*. In the words of Deleuze: 'we don't claim to have written a madman's book, just a book in which one no longer knows – and there is no reason to know – who exactly is speaking, a doctor, a patient, an untreated patient, a present, past, or future patient, (Guattari, 'In Flux', 98). It is generally accepted that this strategy of confusion or indeterminacy never be the case of a psychoanalytic text where the distinction between patient and doctor, clinical vignette and psychodynamic formulation, is of the utmost importance. In a sense, *Anti-Oedipus* undertakes an engagement with psychoanalysis in the most psychoanalytic of ways. The declaration that 'it is at work everywhere' is no less true of the text than it is of an analysand. The arguments one encounters are only one layer in what is ostensibly a flow of associations that need to be listened to analytically – as opposed to captured oedipally – as well as read didactically.

As for Deleuze's comment on the voice that speaks the text, we could add to the list of unknown or unknowable characters those of the psychoanalyst, the philosopher, the lover, the political activist, the aesthete, the clown and the historian. If not endless, the list is made up of at least a thousand different characters with unpredictable and cacophonous voices. Clinically, the picture that (adult) psychoanalysis has trained us to construct is altogether different as the list has remained essentially finite; in fact, it has rarely gone beyond the magic number of five: analyst, analysand, mother, father and child – each as both historical figure and function. According to this latter schema, one could in fact articulate the basic task of the treatment as accomplished when each member of the cast has been given his or her due, and nothing but, when, in other words, the analysand is in a position to distinguish and integrate, cognitively and affectively, the histories, contributions and responsibilities of each member of that cast.

It is no wonder that the initial psychoanalytic encounter with *Anti-Oedipus* cannot but be fraught with risks and tensions. As with its authors, the characters that populate the book, the proper names, the concepts, the events, are too many to keep track of, too singular to categorize, and yet too relevant to dismiss. One is overwhelmed, flooded even. One could cut the treatment short, make a referral or simply write a prescription. One could wade through the details as quickly as possible in order to reach the safety of a working diagnosis or a hook that will order the material and render it more intelligible.[52] One could break through the author–reader distinction and allow oneself to be taken up by the supposed operationality of the book; in other words, one could perform what some psychoanalytic circles advocate as a 'joining'.

Or, and this is the most difficult of options but, I would argue, the one closest to the material, one could approach the text as a training ground where one's ability to juggle and to traverse is rediscovered and honed. Of psychoanalysis, Guattari writes that it 'should simply give you a boost of virtuosity, like a pianist, for certain difficulties. It should give you more freedom, more humor, more willingness to jump from one scale of reference to another' ('So What', 14). Let us note the absence of any notion of 'development' or 'cure' here. Of a psychoanalyst, we already understand and agree to the expectation, nay the demand, not to confuse one history with another, one session with another; not to trail behind the succession of words and events; but not to rush through or pre-empt the flow of experience or affect either. Of *Anti-Oedipus* and its reader, of schizoanalysis, the effect that is anticipated is not one of, at best, attachment and, at worst, allegiance; it is one of agility.

'[W]e are all handymen, each with his little machines' (*AO*, F7 E1). Freud, and much to the chagrin of many of his followers, was a consummate intellectual and clinical handyman. The researcher and experimenter pleasured in constantly expanding the base and scope of his work by relating it to, or incorporating in it, the findings of other disciplines, even if they were unsympathetic to his project and regardless of the resulting tensions: history (cultural, military and archaeological), mythology, literature, physiology, sexology, cell biology. Freud had insisted that psychoanalysis is not a closed system but an incomplete and always modifiable set of interventions ('Two Encyclopaedia Articles', 152). If psychoanalysts could overcome the initial affront of seeing their work, expertise, and long training reduced to the productions of the tinkering handyman and do-it-yourselfer, they might read in the words of Deleuze and Guattari something that is appeasing, if not welcoming. Lacanians might very well endorse the rejection of a developmental understanding of cure; neo-Kleinians recognize not so much the deployment of the notion of partial objects but the value of the ability to recover from one position (the paranoid-schizoid) in favour of another (the depressive); for Winnicottians, the echo of the primacy of play, that which Deleuze and Guattari refer to as *bricolage*, would be most appreciated.

There is much that remains to be said for these points of contact and identification. More importantly however, and as I will show in the next chapter, *Anti-Oedipus* possesses a momentum that distinguishes it from all of these perspectives, a momentum that cannot be subsumed under the formalist logic of the incest-murder paradigm, a momentum that is far from being incapacitated or pathologized by either psychotic rigidity or neurotic doubt, a momentum, finally, in which history and production are invariably at work.

Chapter Four

Process notes: productions and syntheses

To read *Anti-Oedipus* analytically as well as didactically, as I have proposed in the previous chapter, requires that a space be set aside for what are commonly known as process notes among the clinicians. Process notes occupy that space in between the analysand's associations and the analyst's formulations; they do not, properly speaking, belong to a medical record and, unlike the clinical vignette or the case history, they are rarely meant for public consumption. As process notes, the following pages track one reader's impressions as elicited by *Anti-Oedipus*; they are hence as much about that reader as about the text he reads; however, they are neither exhaustive nor conclusive. If and when they analyse, they analyse the text as a movement rather than a meaning; their concern is hence not with the unconscious of the two individuals who authored the text, but with a flow of associations that is not always linear. While they may not always conform to a prescribed standard of thought (continuity, consistency, authority), they do not pretend to defy, transgress or liberate. They are process notes; as such, they occupy that space in between the verbatim of the text and the theory of its interpretation.

* * *

At first glance, the schizoanalytic declaration that 'it' is at work everywhere seems to be perfectly in line with the classic Freudian tenet that the unconscious is, indeed, a dynamic agency whose presence and influence are ubiquitous.[53] However, it is in terms of their assessment of the nature of the dynamism as well as the particulars of its influence that Deleuze and Guattari differentiate themselves from Freud. Following Marx's itinerary in the introductory pages to the *Grundrisse*,[54] Deleuze and Guattari understand human reality as 'universal primary production' (*AO*, F11, E5). Individuals, institutions, theories, body-parts, texts – in short, machines – participate in this production as they emit, circulate and consume infinite and multi-layered flows. Alongside stock markets and consumer goods, production encompasses psyches, structures and affects; it is as relevant to the study of the unconscious as it is to economics. Presumably, this schizoanalytic understanding is in contradistinction to the unconscious Freud had articulated. The one is productive, original and unpredictable while the other is structural, representational and repetitive; the one is grounded in a rich yet disorganized reality while the other is mired in an impoverished and regimented illusion.

What is striking about schizoanalysis is that it differentiates itself not only in terms of the theory it advocates but also, and perhaps most poignantly, in terms of the process by which the theory is conceived and registered. Indeed, and whereas psychoanalysis has sought to distinguish, categorize and classify, to, in other words, determine, schizoanalysis thrives on a reflexivity that permeates its concepts and multiplies its references. Take production for instance: it is never simply the process by which an 'object' is brought into being and then possibly consumed. Production is constituted along three different axes (production, registration, consumption) each of which is transformative of both itself and of the other two. A by no means exhaustive list of illustrations includes those moments when production consumes a raw material or an already existing product in order to attend to its task; when production produces consumption as it creates, shapes and magnifies a demand for its output; when production registers its product in order to claim it for itself as in a trademark; when the registration in turn produces a product as with the record of a thought or a tune, but also, and most significantly, as with the certificate of a citizenship, of a marital or criminal status, of a pathology.[55]

Production is the production of a producing, consuming and registering product; production, in sum, is the production of production. Capital for instance has come to be not only the product of industry, but also the registering surface (as standard of reference) and the driving force (as investment) behind much of human interaction – markets and divisions of labour are but two of its manifestations. Deleuze and Guattari's recruitment of an economic model as the guiding principle of their definition of production might seem a bit odd considering that their project's title announces itself under the register of the psychoanalytic – even if it is *anti*-psychoanalytic – and hence, presumably, the individual and the 'private'. It would appear that Deleuze and Guattari's strategy is the tell tale sign of their having already decided to abandon their clinical audience much as Nietzsche before them had abandoned his philosophical one.[56]

* * *

The assertion that production is the production of production is not without its reverberations in psychoanalysis. The analysand's chain of free associations is not simply a representation of an underlying dynamic, a metaphor for latent peculiarities, or a symptom of as yet undisclosed, or only circuitously disclosed, conflicts and demands. In its vagaries and detours, this chain is a machine whose flow is registered and consumed by an ear, be it that of the analyst or the analysand. It produces an effect, an impression and an experience that, in turn will engender further associations and impressions. To speak of psychoanalysis is to speak of a journey along a complex and multi-layered network of such chains. At best, and though the analyst may be familiar with the terrain, it is the analysand who also steers the process, decides which nodes or junctions to traverse, or, better still, which nodes or junctions to create in order to traverse. The analyst has no way of telling in advance how the adventure will unfold, let alone end, for it is the analysand's as well. The couch disencumbers both from some of the weight of identification. I close my eyes as my analysand's sounds become my images, thoughts, intensities, not so much of where or what she's been but of what she is now making of where or what she thinks she's been. It is not she that I see through her words but what she produces in me, which is not entirely me. What I say, if I say anything at all, and what I do not say, what of all that I do not say she chooses to hear, may or may not link up with what she already sees, thinks and experiences. The flows of words, hers and mine, are products that not only register (speak) pre-existing, and hence consumable (heard) identities, understandings and affects; they also produce further associations and understandings.

In this context, a machine or a chain of associations works only when it breaks down (*AO*, E8). It works by breaking down, continually, by having the flow it produces interrupted and consumed by another that is inevitably produced by it. 'Breaking down' in the French original is actually *detraquée* (*AO*, F14), and the word suggests not so much a cessation of work but the impression of something gone awry, derailed, a loose screw perhaps. The 'derailing' of a machine is tantamount to the detours of slips, dreams and symptoms that psychoanalysis has rightly marked as not only proofs of the unconscious but also products of its inner workings. Slips, dreams and symptoms are not simply the breakdowns of reason, grammar or memory they seem to be; they are the formations the unconscious produces so that it may negotiate its tensions and conflicts. The question that has so far preoccupied psychoanalysis has been the identification and resolution, or at least containment, of the conflict that underlies any particular formation through a retrograde analysis that will trace it back to its earliest possible scenarios. Schizoanalysis, however, marks such formations as not only effects but causes and machines as well. How can they be re- or differently aligned? What can they be made to produce? To what new sounds, significations or formations do they point? The question of effect and machine is always double: 'Given a certain effect, what machine is capable of producing it? And given a certain machine, what can it be used for?' (*AO*, F8, E3).

* * *

A machine is never on its own. One (the machine – the author, the mother, the analysand, for instance) is not the originary number. A machine is always producing of a flow, of a product. Two (the machine and its flow – author and text, mother and milk, analysand and speech) is not the originary number either. A machine produces not only a product but also a product that is producing of another, that is itself a machine, a consuming machine to be more precise. Three (the machine, its flow and the machine that consumes that flow – author, text and reader; mother, milk and infant; analysand, speech and analyst) is still not the originary number. The presence of a machine presupposes not only another that it produces but yet a third by which it had been preceded and produced, and so on. Infinity is the originary number. The presence of a machine is made possible only in an infinite series or string (and . . . and . . . and . . .) of connecting, producing, consuming and registering machines. Governed by such a 'connective synthesis', the series itself can exist only in an immensely complicated matrix or network of production among whose components we may count sexuality, kinship, market forces, intellectual histories, legal and juridical constraints, scientific and aesthetic achievements and physiological contingencies. Ultimately, meaning resides in such activities; it is neither assumed as a structural origin nor is it deferred till the moment of a product or an end.

The clinical implication here is threefold:

- First, the distinction between reality and unconscious phantasy, between what belongs to the everyday and what is 'properly' psychoanalytic, is in the understanding of the relationships and events between machines and not in their presumed locations or determinations, in, for instance, their relations of production, registration and consumption rather than in the extent to which they do or don't correspond to 'actual' or 'reasonable' objects. We shall soon see the work of this distinction in the context of what Deleuze and Guattari term schizophrenic process and social delirium.
- Second, the notion of termination as cure, truth, or position is never truly 'terminal'; the connective synthesis is endless in its dynamic and the clinical concern, as indeed it has now become for many, is much less with

an end to a process than it is with its extension and deployment beyond the point where the presence of the analyst is mandatory.

- Third, and perhaps most disruptively, if, for psychoanalysis, Oedipus is our fate, a given and a universal that may be witnessed, registered and understood while nothing much of it can be altered, for schizoanalysis, Oedipus is a product and, in turn, not only the process by which certain repressions, pleasures and differences are produced and put into place but also the effect of prior processes and machines and hence subject to the interventions and modifications of future processes and machines; its immutability is suspect.

* * *

'Universal primary production' (*AO*, F11, E5) is how Deleuze and Guattari understand the reality of man and nature, not so much as a self-propelled and all-consuming web of production that is in and for itself but as a matrix along whose intersecting series much is produced and much is interrupted. The distinction here is delicate and yet crucial. Production is the fundament of human reality and not its goal. It is the failure to recognize this distinction that leads to ossification and collapse. A process is begun and with it there emerges the tendency to transform it into an end in itself. Machinic production (the production of production) is subordinated to the logic of the production of a whole, a family, an institution or a discipline, which is to say of a perpetually ever-increasing web of functionaries or organization of bureaucrats.

Psychoanalysis, as an institution and as a practice, is an acutely poignant example here. It has suffered from the symptomatology that is typically associated with the schizophrenic found in mental institutions: 'an autistic wreck' (*AO*, F11, E5) hell bent on its own perpetuation and propagation. Is it any surprise that while this 'wreck' that has been romanticized by much of what has come to be known as 'anti-psychiatry' is precisely what Deleuze and Guattari are not advocating? In any case, and in the context of most of what falls under the heading of psychoanalysis as an institution, clinical and/or theoretical, what we witness today is the dogma and sectarianism that surround the discipline's main figures (from Freud, to Lacan, to Klein, to Winnicott, to Kohut) and the paranoia with which their practices have been engulfed and structured. As we know it and live it, the psychoanalytic institution is dangerously close to becoming its own end, to possessing the main characteristics of what Guattari has termed a 'subjected group', a group that withdraws into itself as it suffers the mechanisms of scapegoating, leaderships, identifications, suggestions, interdictions and disavowals ('The Transference', 62).

Clinically, even Freud in his later years was quite concerned with the interminable practice that psychoanalysis had become. Leading nowhere, the analyst's directive to 'go ahead and speak' has produced little other than the family circle and the figure of Oedipus. Under the heading of 'cure', we have come to observe those mechanisms of identification and internalization designed to guarantee in the analysand the reproduction of the analyst as healthy norm. Under the heading of 'no cure', we instead observe the dislocation of a process from the supposedly trivial concerns of the everyday and its transformation, even elevation, into a goal, into something to be pursued 'for its own sake'. In either case, the breakdown in machinic production is palpable. Of course, psychoanalysis is not unique in this respect. The discourses of the academy and the theoretical sciences have fallen prey to exactly the same dynamic.

* * *

The reflexivity that is the marker of schizoanalysis pertains not only to the concepts that *Anti-Oedipus* communicates (as, presumably, the 'products' of its authors' intellectual labours) but also to the ways in which these concepts are registered and consumed, to, in other words, the effects these concepts produce in their registrations and consumptions. In a first moment, each of these concepts is a machine that, like any other for Deleuze and Guattari, refers not to a meaning but to the set of uses and effects it may generate. Each belongs to a series of machines that are often disparate and at times even inappropriate (read: without the proper 'clinical', 'philosophical' or 'economic' credentials): Büchner, Beckett, Artaud, Bataille, Lawrence, Miller, Michaux, Lindner. In their style, the series are declarative, brisk, uncompromising; there is hardly anything ponderous to their tone, there is even less that is smooth to their flow. They run, they halt, they grate and then they pick up again. The obstacles and pitfalls are potentially numerous here; they echo the movements and breakdowns of the machines of which they speak, of the unconscious of which both they and their Freudian counterparts continue to speak. I shall highlight other moments of this reflexivity as they become more explicit.

In the meantime, talk of uses brings us face to face with the question of the 'applications' and 'politics' of *Anti-Oedipus*. That such a question is already a pressing one is supported by two separate yet interconnected factors, the one situational and the other textual. *Anti-Oedipus* was written as a product of and a response to a time when most Western European intellectuals were pressured, yet again, to lead or at least to speak on behalf of a universal subject embodied by the state, the party or the downtrodden. Deleuze often recounted the times when his lectures at Vincennes were met with incomprehension and hostility for having failed to provide such guidance or voice; he, of course, was not alone in his predicament. Foucault, Adorno and Lacan, among many others, were repeatedly pressured with the demand for leadership and/or representation. Nor is this demand specific to a period of crisis or upheaval as was the case within the intellectual circles of the late 1960s. Indeed, one could argue the ubiquity of the logic of demand and its corollaries debt and exchange. That something in the order of the economic permeates much of human activity, including the intellectual and the psychoanalytic, is often acknowledged but rarely utilized.[57]

In this light, a defence for Deleuze and Guattari's resistance to the question of application is that their text is merely a blueprint: 'guess, given its geometrical description, what a knife rest is used for' (*AO*, F8, E3). The description is assumed to point to a product that in turn points to a multitude of uses many of which have yet to be produced. While this may very well be the case, it is not the only case. Indeed, *Anti-Oedipus* is not merely a 'geometrical description' pointing to a yet unknown political organization, theoretical style or clinical practice; it itself is a product whose provocative, unmediated and unmediating tone has engendered a reception reverberating with the echoes of the clinically borderline with its attendant splits between love and hate, idealization and dismissal. Deleuze and Guattari's concern was primarily with what an event or a machine can potentially produce. In a 1983 essay on psychoanalysis and everyday life, Guattari focuses on the 'myths of reference' as they are to be judged according to their social functionality. Do they work? How do they work? What are they capable of producing? What can they be made to produce? Guattari extends an invitation

> to all parties and groups concerned, in accordance with the appropriate modalities, to participate in the activity of creating models that touch on their lives. Furthermore, it is precisely the study of these modalities that . . . [is] the essence of analytic theorizing. ('Psychoanalysis Should Get a Grip on Life', 72)

It is what happens after the theory and the event have taken place that is most relevant; as everyone is trying to overcome the shock, the revolution or the interpretation, it is to what they may make possible and to what may succeed them that Deleuze and Guattari will pay the most attention. Rather than outcomes or recapitulations of the past, these are breakdowns and interventions that redirect a flow toward its future possibilities. Historically, *Anti-Oedipus*, as produced by, among other things, the intellectual organizations and breakdowns of the late 1960s, will in turn generate its own concepts and breakdowns.

* * *

We witness near the closing of the chapter's first section what might seem like a moment of dialectical abstraction: 'desiring-machines make us an organism; but at the heart of this production, within its very production, the body suffers from being organized in this way, from not having some other organization, or no organization at all' (*AO*, F14, E8). Deleuze and Guattari seem to be telling us if not the truth of production then at least the truth of one of its vicissitudes. Presumably, the linear series of production, registration and consumption congeal enough to produce their own antithesis: the non-productive dis-organization that is the 'body without organs'. To some, this may sound shockingly, perhaps even distastefully, Hegelian. Hardly, since the production of the body without organs does not carry with it any evidence of finality; qualitatively, it is eruptive and unpredictable.

* * *

While there is much in it that tells us what it does, there is nothing in *Anti-Oedipus*, so far at least, that explains what a body without organs is; instead, we are told what it is not. The body without organs is neither a projection nor a metaphor; in fact, it has nothing to do with the body or with an image of the body; it is not the residue of a lost totality, which suggests that it is without origin; and it has no productive quality whatsoever, which also suggests that it has no use or purpose (*AO*, F14, E8). Such a concept sounds utterly incomprehensible, indigestible; it is a wrench in the wheel of the reader's interpretive organization; it is the moment of incomprehensibility, or anti-comprehensibility, that halts the production and flow of meaning between author, text and reader; it is the moment at which the text ceases to yield. In the second moment of its reflexivity, and as a theory of the body without organs, *Anti-Oedipus* registers and hence produces that which it theorizes; it is also the process by which it becomes what it theorizes. It not only theorizes the impossibility of imaging, producing a copy, whether good or bad, of the body without organs, it itself becomes such a body; it is unavailable for copying. Any attempt at reproducing in its totality a theoretical image of this body, including the one I am currently undertaking, is bound to be unproductive, or productive of another extension of the same organ-less body, or of an altogether different body.

* * *

If one accepts this schema of the connective synthesis and its relationship to the body without organs, then, and in opposition to the many commentators who have read the '*Anti-*' in the book's title as a final and unequivocal negation of the psychoanalytic project, I would like to suggest instead that this '*Anti-*' echoes what Deleuze and Guattari have termed anti-production. Production halts as the machines respond to the suffering caused by what is essentially a stabilizing 'the way things are is the way things ought to be' dictum. The 'body without organs' emerges as unmediated anti-production; it is neither the starting point nor the culmination of the process; it is only a moment in it. Though unproductive, it is produced by a certain organization of the machines and, soon after its appearance, the flows do resume and the relationships between machines and bodies do multiply. Similarly, and in one of its moments, *Anti-Oedipus* stands to psychoanalysis in the same relationship that the body without organs does to desiring machines; it is neither the primary nor the final word on the psyche; it is produced by, and hence contingent upon, the rigid over-organization of the machines of psychoanalysis as they have constituted a clinical practice and a theoretical enterprise; it is the point at which said organization halts. It is unproductive, which is not to say irrelevant; it is a moment in the series of events, structures and organizations that think and write the unconscious; its effects are neither universal nor static and its final word has not been and, thankfully, never can be spoken; the machines and series in which it participates will invariably regroup and the desire that thinks, writes and analyses will circulate once again. While a mark of opposition, the '*Anti-*' is then neither a repudiation nor a substitution; it is the index of a sequence and a challenge.

* * *

I would like to underscore the quality of a Lacanian imaginary in the reader's relationship to the text, not as analyst but as object for an attempt at a so-called analytic reading. Indeed, and at one level at least, we have both a duplication and a reversal of the analytic process. One approaches a text expecting it to provide knowledge much like one approaches an analyst as the subject supposed to know. As the reader reads, the text effects the analytic move of thwarting interpretation and unsettling those demands imposed upon it under the register of the textual imaginary: unity, structure and meaning. As a body without organs, the text repels its reader's organization of words and concepts and forces her or him into a confrontation with and an accountability for the basic tenets of readership. I would like to suggest that the awareness that a reversed scenario is also at work in the clinical setting is critical. The analysand approaches the analyst as a repository of knowledge and an instrument of relief, as, in other words, a subject supposed to know who, ostensibly, knows little and, in knowing that little, is most frustrating. Meanwhile, the analyst has already, qua analyst, approached the analysand as the subject in whose depths lies a set of truths that have yet to be consciously known, truths in whose name no resistance is justifiable. Lacanians pride themselves on the fact that what distinguishes them from the rest of their analytic counterparts is their refusal to be entrapped in the imaginary logic of the counter-transference. Their wager is that such a refusal affords them a better focus on the analysand's symbolic underpinnings; in the process, their wager blinds them to the reality of the presence of at least two often equally thwarting imaginary registers in the room.

* * *

I would like to return to the question of theory, its practices, applications, links and dislocations. What is the theory of the body without organs that is being proposed in the opening pages of *Anti-Oedipus*? What is its basis? Can one speak of it as having a basis at all? The first synthesis, the connective (and . . . and . . . and . . .) synthesis of production, the producing/product identity, implicitly suggests what Deleuze had to spell out later on in his conversation with Foucault on the logic of 'Intellectuals and Power'. The duality theory/practice is a producing product Deleuze insists; practice is invariably informed and driven by an often implicit but not any the less potent set of theoretical presuppositions while theory is a practice whose laws and dynamics are subject to transformation and interruption ('Intellectuals and Power', 205–07). This question of the duality theory/practice is by no means specific to the fields of political participation or psychoanalytic intervention. Indeed, a reordering of the axioms of scientific priority governing experience and observation is part of what propelled the break that quantum mechanics produced in relation to relativity theory in the mid-1920's. Einstein and Schrödinger had abstracted from the phenomena of observable daily experience imagery that they then reinterpreted for the atomic realm. The macroscopic experience of two like-charged billiard balls repelling each other was transferred onto the atomic domain to explain the behaviour of electrons (Figure 1). Likewise, the atom itself was understood and represented as a minuscule solar system with its own internal gravitational dynamics (Figure 2). In this model, experience and its figurative representation are imposed onto the theory; they shape it and ground its claim to truth. With his quantum mechanics, Heisenberg quickly came to challenge relativity theory on the basis of reality's inherent discontinuity and dubious causality; he insisted that neither could be accurately visualized or known. Heisenberg argued that mathematical abstraction must precede any diagrammatic representation and it in fact took 23 years (from 1925 to 1948) for such a representation to catch up and make its presence felt on stage. Feynman's diagram of two electrons producing a light quantum (Figure 3) could not have been drawn without the mathematical formulations of quantum mechanics. The difference between Figures 1 and 3 is twofold: the first is in the order of priority (experience/ representation versus theory); the second – the one of particular interest to me at this point – is in the nature of the representation itself; Figure 1 is the

FIGURE 1

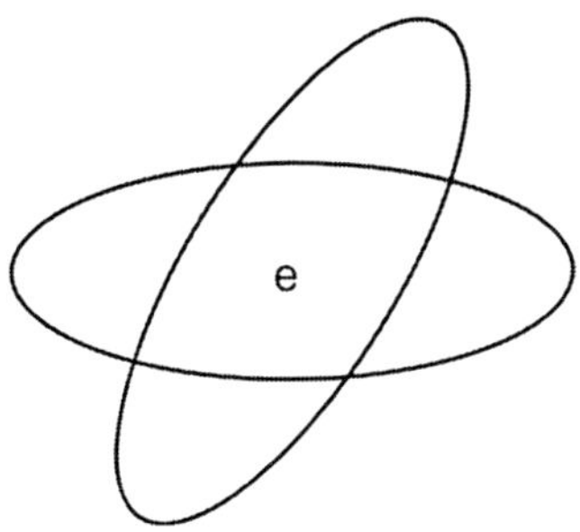

FIGURE 2

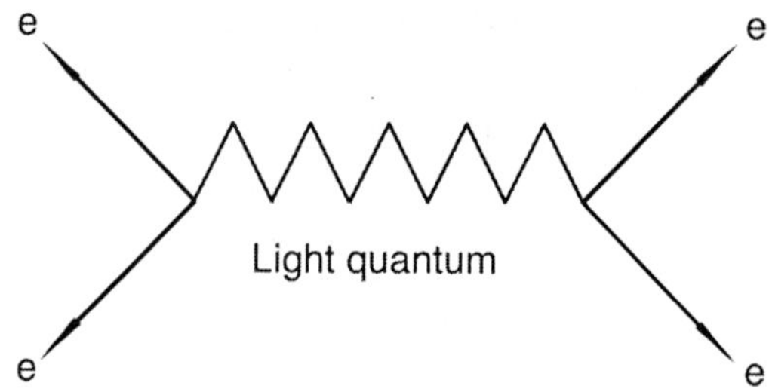

Figure 3

image of two objects in motion, whereas Figure 3 is the schema of a light quantum as an event between two unrepresentable objects.

Much like Einstein, Freud relied on the accounts of everyday life to ground and shape his theories. And just as much as relativity theory extrapolated patterns of experience from the macroscopic onto the atomic, Freud relished his incursions into anthropology and archaeology in order to draw homologies between the developments of the species (phylogeny) and those of the individual (ontogeny). The Platonism that quantum mechanics has come to reflect, the idea that mathematics is the true language of nature, is echoed in Lacan's investment initially in topological constructs and subsequently, in the last decade of his career, in the formulae that were meant to encapsulate the workings of the unconscious: the mathemes.[58] These mathemes were designed to achieve at least two things: first, to bridge the gap between word and experience and hence make possible the transmission of knowledge, specifically, psychoanalytic knowledge; and, second, to redress the confusion to which both word and experience must inevitably give rise.

In positing the mathemes, Lacan claimed to have evacuated subjectivity, and especially his own subjectivity qua master of a theory and guardian of a practice, from the core of psychoanalytic knowledge.[59] Each formula is supposed to acquire a reading only in its use; each is created in order 'to allow for a hundred and one different readings, a multiplicity that is acceptable as long as what is said about it remains grounded in its algebra' ('The Subversion of the Subject', 301). Ironically, it did not take long for the mathemes as a formalization of psychoanalytic knowledge, as, in other words, the theory and signpost of a practice, to become the gatekeeper that normalizes access to both the theory and the practice. In the words of Jacques-Alain Miller, Lacan's son-in-law, heir to the throne and the spokesperson of the hyper-logical strain in Lacanism: 'the thesis of the matheme thus implies that only an effective engagement in an original work pursued within or on the basis of the Freudian field will henceforth constitute credentials for the exercise of a function in the department' (quoted in Roudinesco, *Jacques Lacan & Co.*, 570). This injunction was circulated in 1974; the department in question was the recently established Department of Psychoanalysis at Vincennes; no mere metaphor, the Freudian Field was indeed the title of the influential psychoanalytic series published by the Editions du Seuil under the directorship of Lacan. Both department and book series were soon to be taken over by Miller.

* * *

While in the early 1970s quantum mechanics began to give way to yet another of the twentieth century's most influential theories in physics – chaos theory, – Lacanism, under its newfound banner of the matheme, had reached its own moment of anti-production and thus began to give way to chaos itself. Pontalis, Laplanche and Guattari had already left the master's camp; Leclaire and Irigaray were soon to follow. As well, Lacan's Ecole freudienne was plagued by schisms that soon led to the proliferation of various dissident groups that would challenge the master's authority, analytically and institutionally; the Quatrième groupe, under the leadership of Jean-Paul Valabrega, is among the most notable of these.[60] All of this was precipitated in part at least by the rise of the hyper-logical tendency and the increased control its champion, the dreaded Miller himself, was to have over the various branches of the Lacanian field: the text of Lacan's seminar, the training institute, the academic department, and finally the publishing arm.

My incursion into this bit of intellectual and institutional history helps me situate *Anti-Oedipus* not only within the psychoanalytic context but also within that of one of the most central intellectual concerns of the twentieth century. Deleuze and Guattari were by no means impermeable to the pleasures and pressures to take sides in the experience versus abstraction debate: Einstein/Heisenberg, Freud/Lacan.[61] However, Deleuze and Guattari opted for the third possibility, the one that neither physics nor psychoanalysis had acknowledged. I am referring here to that possibility one finds in Nietzsche's works as I have read them in the first chapter.

In *The Logic of Sense*,[62] Deleuze had pointed out that Nietzsche's principal philosophical project, his so-called reversal of Platonism, did not consist in the privileging of experience at the expense of abstraction since Plato himself never did dismiss experience in the first place. What the Greek philosopher had actually done was to prioritize among the various experiences in order to distinguish between the good copies of the ideal and universal Forms from their bad and cheap imitations. Nietzsche's reversal of Platonism is effected only when the distinction good copy/bad copy and the system of reference upon which it is based (the Form) have been dismantled. Here, the antithesis of the duality true world (Form) and apparent world (copy) is ostensibly the duality of world and nothing (*The Will to Power*, #567). Consequently for Nietzsche, and as I have already presented, 'coming to know means "to place oneself in a conditional relation to something"; to feel oneself conditioned by something and oneself to condition it – it is therefore under all circumstances establishing, denoting, and making-conscious of conditions (not forthcoming entities, things, what is "in-itself")' (*WP*, #555). The world we know is a world of conditional relations and not of objects. Stripped of such relations, it ceases to exist. Translated into Deleuzo-Guattarian terms, these relations are not to be understood in causal terms; rather, they are to be subsumed under the heading of a machinic production and its reflexive corollaries.

Had Heisenberg read Nietzsche? I do not know. However, and notwithstanding his will to abstraction, the physicist recognized that the thing-in-itself – the electron – could not be represented and was hence experientially unknowable in itself. Feynman's diagram is again the schema of an event, of a conditional relation of repulsion between two electrons. We do know that Freud had in fact read Nietzsche and that he had developed a conditional relation of envy and resentment toward the philosopher who had intuited the conclusions that he had had to spend an entire lifetime observing clinically. We also know that Lacan's conditional relation to the German philosopher was one of admiration: he had read and eulogized his texts as an adolescent and then, after he had completed his medical studies, had been exposed to them once again via Georges Bataille, both at Acephale and the Collège de sociologie. It is rather unfortunate but perhaps not too surprising that envy, resentment and admiration obscured one of Nietzsche's most fundamental insights: what is to be analysed is not the unconscious as a thing in itself, but the relations and the events which constitute it, and that such an analysis must itself figure among these relations and hence be the object of its own analysis.

Of course, both Freud and Lacan, each in his own particular way, made extensive clinical use of such relations and events, especially in their transferential echoes. Invariably however, that use was motivated by an epistemophilic drive whose principal aim was the 'truth' of the analysand's unconscious; the interpretation (Freud) or dialectization (Lacan) of the transference is relevant only insofar as it makes explicit the analysand's psyche in its wishes, histories, structures and frustrations. Even within those other clinical quarters where the reciprocal relational nature of the analytic encounter had been underscored – the so-called two person psychologies of Fairbairn, Klein and Winnicott for instance – the (sufficiently analysed) analyst's share, his or her counter-transference, has been invariably filed under the rubric of the analysand's projective identifications, reverberations or deficits and hence, yet again, pertaining to the supposed truth of the latter's unconscious. While indeed highly useful, such clinical strategies remain bound to the understanding of the unconscious as a discreet and knowable object merely influenced by its relations to other equally discreet objects.

* * *

Consider, for instance, the dynamics of mourning and melancholia as they were first elaborated by Freud and subsequently deployed by Klein as the launch pad for her theorizing the ubiquity of ambivalence. What have remained under-investigated are much less the mourner's responses to the experience of object loss and what these responses betray of his or her psychological structures and strategies, but rather the qualitative transformations in the relations the mourner has had to the supposedly lost object. At the level of the unconscious, neither objects nor relations ever die; they only get transformed. What is experienced is hence not so much the loss of the object but the abrupt reshaping of one's relationship to it. Mourning and melancholia are among the vicissitudes of one's relationship to other relations and not to objects as such. These vicissitudes never occur in a vacuum; they are invariably predicated upon – which is to say produced, registered and consumed by – the current, as well as the long history of, relations of so-called loss the mourner has witnessed, learned and been shaped by. The logic of the connective synthesis is as relevant here as it is in the context of the desiring machines and it is no coincidence that Deleuze and Guattari will speak of the body without organs as the unproductive, unconsumable and imageless 'full body of death' (*AO*, F14, E8). The desiring machines do not cease to exist, with the emergence of the body without organs as death the flow of the connective synthesis is halted momentarily but only to be further reconfigured and organized.

* * *

'We shall not inquire how all this works together: the question itself is the product of abstraction' (*AO*, F14, E8). Again, and of the parallel between desiring production and social production: 'such a parallel is merely phenomenological: it does not prejudge in any way the nature and the relationship of the two productions, not even whether there are indeed *two* productions' (*AO*, F16, E10). *Anti-Oedipus* explicitly and persistently repels any attempt to make it accountable for a specific code, arrangement or meaning. It is no wonder that the barrage of concepts, names, code words and events maintains an excess of speed where one can no longer differentiate between the various components. The text as register reads at the rate of a thousand words per minute; one is left with the taut and opaque barrier of a flat line. Why would a text wish to repel its reader? What are the uses, applications or political lessons implicit in such repulsion? And what losses and/or recuperations are inherent to such uses and applications? These questions make as little, and as much, sense as they would if they were posed of an electron repelling another.

One thing is certain though: the text's initial overarching and forcefully unbending declarations have now given way to a 'slippery' (*AO*, F15, E9) surface on which a traveller, no matter how well trained or properly equipped, cannot but trip and fall. This fall is bound up with Deleuze and Guattari's understanding of primary repression as repulsion, in this case the repulsion of the desiring machines by the body without organs – an understanding which, interestingly enough, is parallel to that of Freud's elaborations on primary repression as the mechanism by which the unconscious is set up as the system that will subsequently endure repression 'proper', secondary re-pression, pressure again ('Repression', 147). In his 1959–60 seminar, Lacan had translated Freud's point in terms of the subject being founded by an act of primary forgetting (*The Ethics of Psychoanalysis*, 43–70). Another version of the question: 'why would a text wish to repel its reader?' would then be: 'why would the subject, why would the I forget?' The answer is that the I is fundamentally incapable of answering such a question for it is not simply the subject of forgetting but its product, as forgetting. Similarly, the body without organs does not choose to repel. It is produced as repelling. In its essence, it is not the planned or hoped for outcome of a project or programme. Much like production, it is not a goal of human activity, but one of its constitutive moments as that tense and conflictual set of relations without which such activity would not be possible in the first place.

I say conflictual because, and as much as we know it as a conditional relation of repulsion, or paranoia as Deleuze and Guattari prefer to think it, we also know the body without organs as a conditional relation of attraction. This is where the parallel, and hence transversality, between desiring production and social production begins to prove itself useful. The body without organs (capital, for instance) flows; it does not produce anything; but it does register onto itself the machines (labour) it initially repelled. It is through that labour that it will get to reproduce itself. Attraction and repulsion do not cancel each other out; they coexist (*AO*, F17, E11). The capitalist is proud of his accomplishments, property, factories and labourers; but he is also adamant on maintaining most of the ideological and economic lines that distinguish him from these labourers. The upshot here is what Deleuze and Guattari term a 'social delirium', a specific type of registration that regulates the flow and fixes it so as to make of capital a god and of labour a so-called 'miraculated' machine that would not have existed without the supernatural powers of such a god and to whom it must henceforth owe its sustenance and value.

* * *

It is in terms of this tension that Deleuze and Guattari understand the fetish, not as a commodity or body part standing in for the absent phallus as, presumably, the only legitimate object of desire, but as the movement, event and relationship that reverse the connective synthesis and fix the machine as fatefully miraculated, as, in other words, owing its existence to some body without organs without which it cannot survive. The logic of Oedipus is a telling example of such a fetish; without it, presumably, sanity is impossible.[63] To put it bluntly, the logic of the fetish here is the intolerant and singular logic of the 'without me, you are noting' that one party fosters and with which another colludes. Author and reader, teacher and student, analyst and analysand, parent and child, ruler and ruled; these are some of the structural couplets that breathe in the stagnant air of resentment without which, and in an ironically doubled and nested move, the corresponding institutions of Literature, Pedagogy, Psychoanalysis, Family, and State would not exist. 'Without me, you are nothing' is the logic of quasi-causes, of boundaries and restrictions, of confinements and regulations through which the leak is construed as a threat and the crossing is supposedly a crossing into illegitimacy, chaos, fragmentation and disintegration.

But it is precisely the impermeable boundary itself that divides, consolidates and reifies the functions of dictator, father and super ego. Often enough, the crossing is not into chaos but into a more liveable and freer sanity. Instead of health or truth, it is territoriality and power that are the fundamental concerns of the institution and its fetish. Ostensibly, this 'without me, you are nothing' is but a thin veil for a deep and desperate projection: 'without you, I am nothing.' To admit that much is to renounce the fallacy of the hierarchy that allows me to identify myself as your superior (in health, truth or wealth); it is to renounce my investment in my phantasy of my superiority over you, which is to say, it is to recognize my aggression toward you as someone I wish to subordinate. Freud's elaborations on projection in the 'On the Mechanisms of Paranoia' chapter of his study on Schreber ('Psychoanalytic Notes', 196–219) still hold true, especially when one inscribes them within the circuit of the conditional relations of the inter-subjective.

In the face of this 'without me, you are nothing', and instead of the all too familiar reversed and hence equally fetishistic and resentful response by the other, Deleuze and Guattari not only insist on the infinitely open quality of the binary series of machines that precludes the fixity of pedigree, they also complicate the situation through the second of the text's syntheses, the disjunctive synthesis (either . . . or . . . or . . .), the production of registration. The surface of the body without organs is taut and smooth. It is without itineraries, or rather, its itineraries are infinite. One can and often does slide and associate from a given point to another in a thousand different ways: either this way, or that, or the other; and on it goes. Contra the logic that demands that the legitimate itineraries be fixed in number and confined by mutual exclusivity (this or that, mother or father, masculine or feminine, homosexual or heterosexual), Deleuze and Guattari identify the infinitely more flexible, but not any the less sensical, disjunctive synthesis (either . . . or . . . or . . .) that explodes the constraints of the sequential and binary order of a rigid linear connection. The trajectory from one machine to another is multiplied and both machines are no longer necessarily connected, and when they are so connected the link is not exclusively through the shortest route that is the straight line. The hold of the linear connections of logic (grammar) and causality (time) is loosened as the disjunctions overlay the connections; both are henceforth inscribed in a multi-dimensional space.

With the disjunctive synthesis, it is linear, chronological time that is most crucially undermined, time as a causal connector and developmental ground for both understanding and intervention, in other words, time as a fetish. For Schrödinger, the cat in the box, the cat we cannot see, is not simply either dead or alive; it is both dead and alive. At the quantum level, thinking the physics of the overlay and simultaneity of the disjunction with the connection has given rise to such notions as superposition and the multiverse without which many of our current technologies would not obtain. While the controversy thrives in scientific circles as to which of these two theories or inscriptions is the more appropriate or justifiable, it would make some sense to suggest that both indeed are equally so, that, as incomprehensible as it may initially seem, simultaneity (of states or of worlds) is not simply a peculiar characteristic of a psychological phenomenon identified by a supposedly long outdated dogma. The unconscious, as primary process, i.e. as a form of thought that stresses the untimely rather than the serial and exclusive, is not contained within the confines of the archaic or the phantastic; it is our reality, physical as well as psychological, at its most elemental and productive.

* * *

A minor but hopefully useful digression regarding the potentials of this multi-dimensionality: for the longest time, sign language was considered a kind of pantomime, a crude iconic code lacking the sophisticated complexities and potentials of language. Its speakers were often relegated to the realm of the childish, pathological or primitive because of their supposedly restricted capacities to communicate and therefore to think symbolically. William Stokoe has thankfully corrected our view. As it turns out, and through its use of the three dimensions of space (from the directionality of its nouns, verbs and adverbs to the perspectival qualities of its narrative) as well as its inscriptions in time, sign language exploits to their fullest certain grammatical and syntactic possibilities that neither speech nor writing can even begin to approximate.[64] The 'deaf and dumb' are so only because most of us the hearing do not have the experiences, or perhaps even the cerebral capacities, to grammaticize space, to use it linguistically,[65] to, in other words, cross into a mode of expression and thought that surpasses the one-dimensional registering of speech or the two-dimensional registering of writing. Is it any wonder then that our civilization has consistently valorized the so-called 'properly' linguistic at the expense of the visual? And is it any wonder that the psychoanalytic field has picked up the bias and extended it to the point where the two-dimensional structure of language (its metonymy and metaphor à la Lacan) and its testimony to a higher capacity to mourn (as a symbolic representation à la Klein and Segal) have colonized our understanding of the unconscious and relegated any non-linguistic presence in the analytic session to the realm of the unmetabolized and acted out resistance or, better still, the symptom of a regression to the so-called 'pre-verbal'? One of the principal effects of language as a machine here is to produce, regiment and prioritize structure over experience, to relocate and devalue the non-verbal as pre-verbal, which is to say infantile. As much as, and hence precisely because, the body is available for verbalisation, it is also, in at least one of its core registers, a body without language, a body whose tremors and passions often cannot be 'spoken'.

* * *

Another note on the translation is in order. Quite critical and most misleading in the English rendering is the translation of *se rabattre sur* (*AO*, F16) as 'to fall back onto' (*AO*, E10). The learned footnote on page 10 of the English text lists the various meanings of the verb 'rabattre' and evokes, whether intentionally or not, the very same mechanisms Freud had discussed under the heading of regression in the seventh chapter of *The Interpretation of Dreams*: temporal, formal, topographical.[66] Indeed, the translators of *Anti-Oedipus* have in mind a return to a preceding position or state as they interpret *rabattre* as a rotation followed by a reverse rotation, as a retreat or as a reduction. But, and if production 'falls back onto' registration, and registration, in turn, 'falls back onto' consumption, this is because, for Deleuze and Guattari, registration is the site where 'something in the order of a subject is located' (*AO*, F22–23, E16). 'Falling back onto' would imply a logic of depth through which the subject grounds the various syntheses of the unconscious while it is grounded by consumption. This could not be any further from the French original. Deleuze and Guattari use *rabattre* in its reflexive form, *se rabattre sur* which means to come to or to reach something: the subject is not the ground for but rather a product of the repulsions and attractions between body without organs and machines; the subject is, in other words, a product of consumption, registration and production. I think it is important to qualify the effect of translating *se rabattre sur* as 'falling back onto' as in itself a falling back onto and a regression, ironically, to the very theory the text is disputing.

* * *

The two syntheses of production are subject to fetishistic manipulation: reversal in the case of connection, and exclusivity in the case of disjunction. The fetish is specific to a social delirium (an 'I think') of an apparent movement of, for instance, the body without organs as cause of all production (capital as cause of labour, Oedipus as cause of psychological structuring) or of a decisive choice between two immutable alternatives (either production or consumption, either conscious or unconscious, either inside or outside, either analyst or analysand). In schizophrenic delirium, the two syntheses overlap; fluidity is the order of the day.

It seems that the schizophrenic passes from one code to the other, that he *scrambles all the codes*, in a quick sliding, according to the questions he is posed, never giving the same explanation from one day to the next, never invoking the same genealogy, never registering the same event in the same way, accepting even, when he is forced into it and he is not irritated, the banal Oedipal code, so long as he can stuff it full of all the disjunctions it was designed to eliminate. (*AO*, F21–22, E15)

The echo here is to Deleuze's *Coldness and Cruelty*, his presentation of von Sacher Masoch from a few years prior to *Anti-Oedipus*, specifically to the contract the masochist draws up and proposes to the other, a contract that takes the form of the Law but is indeed designed to generate all that the Law prohibits.[67] The scrambling of codes in this instance operates on at least two levels: at the level of the author of the contract who gets to prescribe the limits of the scene (stereotypically the active 'top' but in this case the supposedly passive 'bottom') and at the level of the content and intent of the contract (impropriety, un-pleasure). If we are in a position to qualify *Anti-Oedipus* itself as masochistic/schizophrenic then we should expect that everything that has been said so far to be subject to the same shifts and scramblings. What we are offered is an ever growing and ever confusing set of syntheses and much of what follows will depend on our responses to it, on what we make of it.

* * *

Keeping in mind the initial definition of production as production, registration and consumption, a third synthesis is invariably at work, a synthesis of consumption that belongs to a 'subject' that is produced by a registration and that defines itself in terms of the registration it consumes (*AO*, F23, E17). How could a registration produce a subject? To begin with, we have two examples from the history and medicalization of sexuality. In the first volume of his *History of Sexuality*, Foucault has outlined for us the registering of homosexuality from the 1850s onwards and how it has come to produce not only the psychiatric category of the homosexual as pathetic and pathological but also the possibilities for its modern day offshoot: the gay subject. As well, Sandy Stone also given us an image of the registering of the transsexual identity from the 1950s onwards, a registering in which the shoddily researched notion of gender disphoria (being born in 'the wrong body') has seeped from the clinic and into the discourses of psychology, politics and popular culture ('The Empire Strikes Back'). Ultimately, and for us here, the most poignant registering of all is Oedipus itself. As our social delirium and fetish, Oedipus registers incest and patricide as primary. Supposedly, the taboo on incest is designed to curb an already existing wish, and guilt to redress and repair the effects of that wish. Freud was quite persistent on both scores and that is precisely why he could never accept the budding Melanie Klein's position. As far as he was concerned, she had argued that one does not feel guilty because one has murdered one's father but rather that one phantasizes the murder of one's father because one already feels guilty. This made no sense to him.

* * *

In Lacanian psychoanalysis, the psychoanalysis with which Deleuze and Guattari were most suffused, *jouissance* has come to hold pride of place among the categories and constructs. *Jouissance* is neither pleasure nor enjoyment;[68] it is what goes beyond either of these two states. Pleasure for Lacan, and for Freud before him, is a minimum of excitation and its principle is to have as little pleasure as possible, to maintain, at whatever cost, the integrity and stability of its subject. *Jouissance* is what motivates a striving and a going beyond the limits of the pleasure principle, a transgression, a seeking out of more pleasure and hence, and in the process, an endurance of pain. *Jouissance* is that paradoxical pleasure that one derives from the symptom, or the gain from the illness as Freud would think it.[69] Put differently, and whereas pleasure and enjoyment confirm the autonomy and integrity of the subject as an ego capable of deciding rationally and for itself the pleasure it seeks, *jouissance* undermines that ego's search for balance and control; it presses upon it and disrupts its sanctum. Rather than the guarantor of a subject's unity and organization, *jouissance* is its destabilizer.

What of the subject in all of this? If the relations between body without organs and desiring machines are of attraction and repulsion, of miraculating and paranoid machines, the relation between the latter two is of a consuming and 'celibate' machine whose jouissance, 'sexual pleasure', 'volupté', is the motor force behind the conjunctive (it's me and so it's mine . . .) synthesis. Crucial for us here is the difference in the language-word: whereas the 'celibate' (*AO*, E17) evokes constraints and abnegations, the '*célibataire*' (*AO*, F24), the bachelor, is a playful suitor, as with Duchamp's *Large Glass*, hovering on the border between the respectable and the unknown, and hence suspect, that is forever produced as a new alliance between the paranoid and the miraculating, between desiring machines and bodies without organs. In this 'celibate' machine the paranoid and the miraculating reconcile, which is not to say that they cancel each other out. Both persist, but this time alongside a degree of voluptuousness, a creativity of what Deleuze and Guattari refer to as states or zones of intensity. Hallucinations and deliriums are secondary to the experience of such zones: Schreber's 'I experience myself becoming a woman' is projected as a hallucination 'I see my reflection in the mirror as a woman' and introjected as a delirium 'I think I am a woman'.[70] This is where the *I* is located, as the outcome of a state and an intensity, of the lived emotion of having breasts which, incidentally, neither resembles nor represents breasts (*AO*, F26, E19). This is why the education (read: the production of the subject) of a cybernetic neural network like Helen in Richard Powers' *Galatea 2.2*, for instance, cannot but fail for 'in evolution's beginning was not the word but the place we learned to pin the word to' (248), a place, indeed a physicality, that that particular machine had never had and hence a pinning that could never take place. This is also why that other Helen (Hélène Cixous) can 'feel' the truth of the mysteries 'woman' and 'man' but, in a moment of the utmost integrity, admits that she does not know how to speak them truthfully ('Tancredi Continues', 83) since their physicality exceeds its status as product of or subject to the laws of language and its metaphors.

* * *

While the subject does depend on the interaction between intensity (I experience), delirium (I think) and hallucination (I see), it is not the sum total of all three moments or modes; it is an offshoot and a side-effect rather than a unity precisely because it is constantly disrupted by its nature as a subject in *jouissance*. In the space of a few lines (*AO*, F27, E21) Deleuze and Guattari counter a long tradition in both philosophy and psychoanalysis that has insisted on inscribing the subject as primarily grounded in the structures of thought (Descartes) and/or language (Lacan). Whether conscious or unconscious, this subject has deluded itself into thinking in the mode of the fetish that it is at the centre of its various experiences and understandings; that it is separate from the constellation of intensities it goes through. This subject may experience, see, or think this or that but, supposedly, it is neither this nor that; it goes so far as to convince itself that it is greater than both, in charge of both and hence capable of the repression and/or the fulfilment of both. This is what has made it possible for psychoanalysis, if not for much of human research, to gravitate around the question 'what does the subject want?' and its variants 'what does the woman want?' and 'what does the other want from me?' The other here may stand for the state, the friend, the god or whatnot. The other also stands for the analyst as much as it does for the analysand, and for the text as much as for the reader.

Clinically, and no matter how complicated or pained the presentation may be, the working assumption is that the analyst, or an analyst, is in a position to understand, to empathize and/or to facilitate 'the' subject. All parties concerned, variations on the theme notwithstanding, share the assumption that is being undermined and exposed in its moment as a fetish by the text of *Anti-Oedipus*, in both word and deed. On the one hand, the text argues the impossibility of a subject prior to the wanting: as much as the *I* is produced as forgetting, it is also produced as wanting; it does not precede it; it does not choose it; it is it. The series of questions ('what does the subject want?' and its variants, including what has become the pivotal clinical concern as to whether or not to gratify the want once it has been identified) becomes secondary and remote in comparison to the modalities and dynamics of the want itself. On the other hand, the text as an avalanche of concepts and permutations on concepts makes me think it impossible to comprehend it as a coherent communication. Note, I say impossible instead of simply difficult or arduous. The text offers a series of syntheses, structures and topologies that are designed specifically for the reader not to understand, or at least to understand only insofar as they are being made use of successively as intensities. In the process, *Anti-Oedipus* is uncovering itself not as a static representation of a consistent meaning or the communication of a self-contained and systematic theory, in other words as a textual subject, but as a series of vignettes and effects with which the reader has to constantly connect and therefore produce.

* * *

One of the main controversies in the history of the psychoanalytic movement has coalesced around the meaning and relevance of insight as a clinical category. A divide has often separated a more classic epistemic orientation from a concern for the analysand's affective well being which, supposedly, may or may not have much to do with the making conscious of conflicts and/or deficits. Through the conjunctive (it's me and so it's mine . . .) synthesis, Deleuze and Guattari are effectively redefining insight and in the process rearranging the terms if not the relevance of the debate here. The synthesis in question is ostensibly a 'so that's what it is!' moment of insight and a clarity identified by its effect to reorganize radically not only delirium (thought) but hallucination (perception) and intensity (experience) as well. The 'so that's what it is!' is not so much a revelation or an uncovering of the subject to itself but the making of a subject. Instead of simply eliciting in the analysand a greater sense of subjective responsibility, or a greater capacity to tolerate anxiety and its ambivalences, or even a broader affective vocabulary or repertoire, the conjunctive synthesis is essentially traumatic in its quality for it is the signpost of a radical shift in the subject's thought, perception and experience, which is to say in the subject's way of deploying itself, for itself as well as for others. Insight is that rare moment of tremor or, at times, of stillness, in the clinical situation that marks for both analyst and analysand a transformation, not only in understanding but also in being and in relating. However, and whereas the trauma (of war or abuse for instance) dissociates the subject from its experiences, thoughts and perceptions, and in so doing robs it of its agility and ossifies it, insight, analytic or otherwise, multiplies the connections between the components; it produces new registrations, experiences, subjectivities; it makes such multiplications and productions tolerable.

Ultimately, the Deleuzo-Guattarian subject is a product of the conjunctive synthesis (so that's what it is/that's who I am . . .); this subject is a moment in the desiring process; it is produced as desiring; it does not precede desire; it does not choose it; it belongs to it. The subject (be it an individual, a text, a practice, or an institution) is the effect of a particular constellation of forces of attraction and repulsion, which is to say of a surround and a situation. It is hence aleatory since the constellation itself is an effect of the ongoing process of production and its three syntheses. This subject is producible – differently, persistently; it is mutable, agile; its history knows little of linearity or development, of stages or resolutions, and only cursorily so. This subject is situational, transitional. Contra the fetish that ossifies it by subsuming its relations and experiences under the heading of this or that topology or purpose, Deleuze and Guattari offer a more modest and hence potentially more flexible and productive strategy for being, for reading, for intervening. Julia Kristeva's insistence that individuality requires that in every analysand be discovered a distinctly new classification (*New Maladies of the Soul*, 9) and Wilfred Bion's oft-invoked recommendation to enter each session with 'neither memory nor desire', with 'no history and no future' ('Notes on Memory and Desire', 272) in order to best be prepared for that session's specific, i.e. situational, productions strike a similar cord.

The clinical concern is henceforth much less with the correction of a pathological present (as the reiteration of disruptive early childhood patterns) in favour of a pre-established adult (read: integrated) identity, and more with what that present is being made to produce or not produce; with the malleable relations and experiences it makes possible. The present is about much less a state of being than a deployment of being, for it too is a machine. This is not to suggest that the subject does not admit of a history; its past (or future) is a machine that is often called upon as hindsight (or projection) in order to justify or make necessary, and sometimes even more tolerable, a present as an investment or a relation. Nor is this subject lacking in a capacity to observe and hence modify itself; it is not without will, though its will, and by extension its want, revolve around a simultaneously more visceral and more subtle concern than for simple advancement or acquisition. Nor, finally, is this subject stripped of any corporeality; its body belongs to more than one schema or organization.

* * *

Let me draw a parallel, temporarily at least, between Lacan's three registers (the imaginary, the symbolic and the real) and the tripartite structure Deleuze and Guattari identify as the basis for the emergence and understanding of a subject: hallucination, delirium and intensity. The correspondences imaginary/hallucination, symbolic/delirium and real/intensity identify the last of the couplets as the experiential priority without which the other two would be impossible. Lacan and Deleuze and Guattari would agree on this point. They would, however, part company on the status of thought and the logic it betrays. The symbolic for Lacan is immutable. One is born into certain linguistic structures over which one has very little if any control. Rather than the resolution, taming or expansion of unconscious thought processes, the analytic task for Lacan consists in giving such processes expression, in articulating their truth and making them subject in and of such structures. In foregoing the formalist distinction between conscious and unconscious – 'it', after all, is at work everywhere – Deleuze and Guattari disentangle among the various expressions of delirium, of the 'I think' and hence of the symbolic, the schizophrenic from the social. Whereas the Lacanian symbolic, its quality, and the fact of its presence or absence, is beyond modification, Deleuzo-Guattarian delirium is indeed subject to transformation: reversal, exclusivity and ossification. It is worth noting here that schizophrenic delirium is not simply the counterpart or specular image of social delirium since its productive quality lies not so much in a Law that will install and ground an identity, but in a process that will come to (*se rabattre sur*) and produce a subject and a meaning that are residual, aleatory.

One of the many implications to this distinction reflects on the practice of the symbolic community. In the one case, it is a given; in the other it is produced. In the one case, it is the limit that safeguards its members from the threat of psychosis (as the symbolic's Other); in the other, it is the porous boundary through which much is trafficked and much is produced.

* * *

At this point, the translation is encumbered by the move from the German original. Freud's Oedipal trinity is of the *es*/it, the *Ich*/I and the *Über-Ich*/Over-I. While his English translators introduced the 'id', 'ego' and 'super ego', their French cousins remained closer to the original with the *ça, moi* and *surmoi.* It is interesting that the translators of *Anti-Oedipus* chose to comply with the English Freud instead of the French Deleuze and Guattari. 'I', 'me' and 'ego' are the choices among which they alternate for the single word *moi* (without apparent rhyme or reason). Perhaps it was their attempt to bring closer to their audiences a text that sounded strange enough already. Mine is not simply a linguistic concern since, and as we already know, Freud used the term *Ich* to refer, at times, to the self in its totality and, at others, to an agency or a part of that self. While it makes his text difficult to read, Freud's equivocation also suggests that the two senses are codependent, that, in fact, one could not speak of a self, of an *I*, without that part, an ego, that negotiates between the demands of desire, reality and the Law, that, in other words, and for Freud at least, to speak of a self is to speak of an agency that has already been Oedipalized. This is how, and much like his clinical predecessors (Kraepelin, Bleuler and Binswanger), Freud seems to have relied on the 'ego', or its absence, to understand the schizophrenic, or at the very least to understand the schizophrenic as beyond psychoanalytic comprehension, and hence intervention.

To be fair to Freud, in one manner of speaking at least, and to also be more accurate, conceptually as well as clinically, it is not on the ego/*moi* that the possibility of therapeutic psychoanalysis hinges. Rather, it is the capacity for object libido, which is to say for the love of an other, that Freud looked for in his prospective analysands. This is not an insignificant distinction. In classic psychoanalytic terms, the *I* that is capable of love is an *I* that has already been oedipalized; it is an *I* that has passed from ego libido to object libido, from secondary narcissism to the super ego (via the ego ideal). The narcissist, the masochist, the homosexual, the schizophrenic, the woman, in sum anything that is not 'Freud', these are all quite capable of uttering an 'I' but theirs has not been fixed enough by its relationship to the familial axes of Oedipus for it to be curable. It is in its endorsement of this non-Oedipal I/*moi* that Deleuze and Guattari's schizophrenic process is to be distinguished from both Lacanism and Ego psychology. The only 'real' relationship – be it of love, hate or what not – is a relationship of production, of desiring production, of the production of the unconscious. Though he claimed all the names of history, Nietzsche, obviously, did not fail to utter an *I* whenever he fancied it or if it suited his purposes. Similarly, the handyman has rarely hesitated to acknowledge an *I fixed it* even though his primary mode as handyman is of fixing things rather than of claiming for himself the things he has fixed.

* * *

From Plato and through to Hegel, the distinction that has governed the analysis of desire is that of production versus acquisition, with desire invariably subsumed under the heading of the latter. At those rare moments when it did depart from this schema, psychoanalysis could conceive of desire as productive only in terms of an internal or 'psychic' reality, of a fantasy and a mimic, of a representation of the real, desired, and hence lacked object. Deleuze and Guattari offer us the linchpin of a critique of the notion of desire as lack and, by extension, of the subject as lacking, as well as the elements of a desire whose three constitutive moments (production, registration and consumption) are both transitive and reflexive. Paradoxically, the anti-oedipal level of abstraction here opens up the possibility for desire as a machine whose satisfaction is not equivalent to having (consumption) or to being (performance); it is rather a matter of doing, which may include having and being but is limited to neither. This is most evident in the context of the reader's relationship to the text: does *Anti-Oedipus* carry with it a measure of either the descriptive or the prescriptive? The former requires an appeal to neutrality that the text has doggedly resisted: indeed, and rather than on entities, its focus has been on events and relations, and, most importantly, on its and its reader's inevitable implications in them. In the process, the text thwarts that reader's demand for an ethical or clinical guideline since such a demand can be satisfied only in a context whereby the agency that makes it and the agency that fulfils it are identifiable and discrete. If anything, the Deleuzo-Guattarian schema reverses the responsibility for satisfaction; the question that is most pressing now is the one that regards not the text's meaning and application but the reader's experiences of use. Dismantle, rearrange and reassemble; the status of the anti-oedipal schema is that of a machine that is distinguishable from the wanderings of its meta-psychological counterparts; it is not so much that we have an account of psyche, text and institution that can better fulfill our analytic, epistemic or political demands; rather, we are offered and drawn into an understanding that obeys the laws of its own inquiry. If the Deleuzo-Guattarian subject is conjunctive, provisional and indeed situational then, as a textual, theoretical and methodological subject, so are *Anti-Oedipus* and its readers.

* * *

One of the most striking qualities of the Deleuze–Guattarian schema is its trinitarian structure: production, registration and consumption; machine, body without organs and subject; paranoid, miraculating and celibate; connective, disjunctive and conjunctive; and, finally, delirium, hallucination and experience. The question that presents itself at this point is whether such a schema is but the latest in a series of vignettes that articulate the fundamental processes of thought (primary and secondary) Freud and Lacan had already attempted. Are we, in other words, witnessing a departure or simply a reiteration, no matter how varied, of what has been said and done, analytically and otherwise, on numerous occasions already? My first response is that the triangulations of social delirium, be they Oedipal or symbolic, are inherently static and stultifying; their forceful insistence on immutability and universality has now become drone-like and quasi-hypnotic. The schema that Deleuze and Guattari offer instead is grounded in a logic of counter-stability; its structure may be tripartite but, and forever, its modalities are infinite, its meanings multiple and its subjects aleatory.

This logic of counter-stability notwithstanding, *Anti-Oedipus* remains most faithful to Freud's core insights. In the name of flows and machines, the text rejects the Freudian understanding of an unconscious that is representational in favour of an unconscious governed by the three productive syntheses. However, with structural linguistics and its Lacanian appropriations for background, Deleuze and Guattari seem to have essentially recast the Freudian mechanisms of displacement, condensation and secondary revision in terms that, though unsettling, are not any the less psychoanalytic. Indeed, displacement, circulation along the axis of contiguity-metonymy, is now the connective synthesis (and . . . and . . . and . . .); condensation, circulation along the axis of selection-metaphor, is now the disjunctive synthesis (either . . . or . . . or . . .); secondary revision, the arrangement of disparate fragments into commonsensical ego narratives, is now the conjunctive synthesis of a partial subject (so that's what it is . . .).

What remains at issue here is the use of such syntheses. Indeed, Deleuze and Guattari identify a psychoanalytic implementation that is confined to a 'this and that' (mummy and daddy), a 'this or that' (masculine or feminine), and a permanent 'it's me' ego. Deleuze and Guattari advance a schizoanalytic implementation where the connections and the disjunctions operate ad-infinitum and the subjectivities to which conjunctions give rise are transitory. With this in mind, the anti-Oedipal criticism can be reformulated as follows: psychoanalysis has betrayed its own first principle of a dynamic unconscious. It has not gone as far as it can actually go. Guattari stated as much in his notes while preparing the text. In the recently published *Ecrits pour L'anti-Oedipe*, he repeatedly admonished psychoanalysis for reintroducing the subject into the very realm from which it had previously evicted it, for subordinating the unconscious to the logic of unity and coherence, in both fact and therapeutic ideal. For Guattari, there is no 'subject' of the unconscious, or rather, 'the subject of the unconscious' is the subject that has already been produced and registered under the sign of Oedipus: 'we can always call it the subject, but then it is the "subject of repression" and not the "subject of desire". In fact, there is no "subject of desire"; there is a *production* of desire according to a *machine of the sign*' (*Ecrits*, 148). And if it is not Oedipus that is the manifest governing principle, if it is the *objet petit a* as with Lacan for instance, Guattari insists that there is no 'barred' or 'castrated' subject; rather, there are multiple subjectivities that have been glued together into a 'loathsome putty' that has taken the place of the desiring machines (*Ecrits*, 215).

Guattari's final verdict is in: psychoanalysis has so far proven itself incapable of tolerating its own groundbreaking discovery; it is on the verge of becoming little more than an ossified and ossifying secondary revision. In privileging the notion of a primary process, *Anti-Oedipus* restores a discourse of, and on, the unconscious that psychoanalysis has often domesticated or betrayed. *Anti-Oedipus* hence belongs at the heart of the psychoanalytic project; that it rejects the Oedipal schema in which Freud encapsulated his findings makes it less Freudian but not necessarily any the less psychoanalytic.

Chapter Five

Sophocles: under the sign of Nemesis

With an analytic rereading of *Anti-Oedipus* in mind, what is left of the man around whom much of psychoanalysis has gathered its momentum? If we are to follow Deleuze and Guattari, there is nothing to Oedipus beyond the tragic and, by extension, nothing to psychoanalysis beyond a depleted and pitiful version of desire from which we all need to be disencumbered. Here, we are faced with a choice between two mutually exclusive options: either (1) we submit to the presumably immutable laws of incest and parricide and their correspondingly inflexible structures of identity or (2) we reject wholesale anything and everything that has ever been ascribed to the king of Thebes in the name of desire and its productions.

It seems to me that the argument Deleuze and Guattari mount against the Oedipal machine – that it is irrevocably one-dimensional, ossified and exclusionary, that it is utterly useless or useful only insofar as it may be deployed occasionally as a sham or a distraction – suffers from what it itself would identify as a social delirium. If psychoanalysis has failed to live up to its own discovery of an unconscious as a productive and dynamic process, schizoanalysis has failed to live up to its own rendering of that very same discovery. Indeed, the schizoanalytic machine has re-produced, registered, consumed, and, in a presumably triumphant move, defecated the Oedipal flow. Here, it has implemented its three syntheses of production in the spirit of a 'once and for all' that could not be any farther from its privileging of open-ended fluidity. It has deployed its conjunctive synthesis in order to confine Oedipus to a one-dimensional and static ego (as tragic and nothing but); its disjunctive synthesis is henceforth a marker for mutually exclusive intellectual and clinical affiliations (either psychoanalysis or schizoanalysis); its connective synthesis is forever rigid and one-directional (the past is past; there's no need to look back).

In this chapter, I would like to return to the Oedipal script and recover in it a dynamic that extends beyond the limits of tragedy and law, a dynamic that psychoanalysis has failed to recognize and that schizoanalysis, in mistaking the Freudian view for the script's only authoritative interpretation, has not sought to investigate. I will braid three lines of argumentation.

- In the first, I will show how thinking Oedipus as exclusively tragic singles him out as unjustifiably immune to two principal tenets of (psycho/schizo) analysis: (1) the ambivalence that is at the heart of any experience or relation; and (2) the ubiquity of overdetermination as a hermeneutic and clinical strategy.
- In the second line, I will underscore an audience's dis-identification with Oedipus the lawbreaker in order to highlight laughter as a crucial component in a production that is as comically moralistic as it is tragic.
- In the third and final line, I will trace a trajectory in the history of cultural production in which both humour and pathos have served as co-constitutive way stations on a continuum whose expression has been a source of individual pleasure and societal cohesion.

Ultimately, the point of my argument is twofold: (1) I would like to rescue Oedipus, the myth and the man, from the throes of tragedy and inscribe him instead in a much broader gamut of meanings and responses; and, much more importantly (2) I would like to disabuse both psychoanalysis and schizoanalysis from the rigidity of solemn representations, whether they are to be endorsed or refuted, and from the doctrinaire demarcations between their corresponding earnest strategies and desiring momentums.

Ambivalence

In his study of the Italian Renaissance, Jacob Burckhardt recounts one of those anecdotes that are 'true and not true, everywhere and nowhere', in other words, one of those anecdotes that are mythic in quality and function:

> The citizens of a certain town (Siena seems to be meant) had once an officer in their service who had freed them from foreign aggression; daily they took counsel how to recompense him, and concluded that no reward in their power was great enough, not even if they made him lord of the city. At last one of them rose and said, 'Let us kill him and worship him as our patron saint'. And so they did. (*The Civilisation of the Renaissance,* 15)

Aside from its all-too-familiar and perhaps even universal juxtaposition of violence with reverence, what, among the countless of Burckhardt's vignettes, marks this one in particular as both mythic and tragic is, ironically but not too surprisingly, the hefty quotient of laughter its recounting often evokes. At another time and in another place, Franz Kafka's reading of his own quasi-mythic tales of humanity's despair and absurdity elicited a similar laughter from his Prague audiences; ditto of the response of many a theatre-goer to the performances of Eugène Ionesco's despairing *La Cantatrice chauve*. Let us not forget Emily Dickinson, that mistress of suffering, who could not but delight in the humorous nuances of certain stories of death and decapitation.

One could easily argue, as is customary nowadays, that, sadism and misanthropy aside, operative in these and most other comic responses is a concealment of and a shield against the poignancy, if not the pain, of the myth and its truth, that, ultimately, the laughter is the very confirmation of what it tries to deny. With pain as the normatively posited response, no psychoanalytic clinician or theorist, to my knowledge at least, has entertained the possibility of a reverse and yet equally vital scenario whereby laughter is the target of concealment and tears are its limpid and unadorned but no less obscuring cover.

And yet, throughout much of its history, psychoanalysis has rightly insisted on the inherently conflicted relationship a subject has with its object. Freud considered the perversions as always paired in the individual: sadism and masochism, exhibitionism and voyeurism are not simply the terms we attach to the separate but presumably complementary roles we adopt in our sexual scenarios, they are co-extensive components of our identities as desiring subjects. As much can be said of femininity and masculinity for what Freud had termed primary 'bisexuality' in his 'Three Essays' of 1905 is better captured in our current lexicon as primary 'bigenderism'. Klein made the case for a similar dynamic, though hers were much starker terms: sexuality and aggression, love and hate, are our inexhaustible rudiments and much of what we know of the unconscious and its positions is articulated through the ways in which the two are lived and negotiated. As for Lacan, that master of the triad wherever registers, passions and diagnoses were concerned, he too insisted on the co-valence of the oppositional pair whenever he addressed technical questions of presence and absence, speech and silence, inside and outside. Deleuze and Guattari, and as I have outlined in the previous chapter, were hardly immune to the selfsame logic: desiring machines versus bodies without organs, miraculating machines of attraction versus paranoid machines of repulsion, social delirium versus schizophrenic process, etc.

Puzzling then is the psychoanalytic refusal to detect anything other than the tortured and tragic in the myth of Oedipus. Puzzling is the discipline's refusal to grant its hermeneutic key, or non-key as the case may be, access to its much-treasured logic of duality and opposition, a logic that would uncover in the Oedipal script its constitutive roots in the humorous. No doubt, the clinical commitment to the alleviation of human suffering has often left little room for the consideration of anything other than the stifling and the traumatic. Indeed, there has been much seductive sense to the argument that the time for laughter and, in this case, personal freedom is possible only after the working through of blockages and inhibitions has been accomplished.[71] Still, and by that very same token, the zeal and earnestness with which psychoanalysis has championed the story of the erstwhile king of Thebes as the embodiment of pathos and nothing but is itself the symptom of an inhibition that is in bad need of analysis and alleviation, an inhibition that is all the more potent precisely because of its silence and opacity, an inhibition that functions in the style of an 'enigmatic signifier' (to borrow the term from Jean Laplanche) and hence of a constitutive communication, in this case of a clinical guideline, that remains unconscious to both sender and receiver, a communication that operates in the mode of a yet unspoken eleventh (psychoanalytic) commandment: *Thou shall not laugh.*[72]

A man, weak in the ankles but strong in combat, politics and love, is doomed to a life of wandering because of the crimes his strengths had afforded him. Aimless, he reaches a sacred ground; blinded, he sees the truths that had previously eluded him. Those he had rescued will come to suffer the most abominable of deaths; those he had opposed will ultimately triumph and prosper. While many of his innocent subjects will have perished of pestilence, our parricidal and incestuous hero, our criminal *par excellence*, will die serene and wise at a ripe old age. Previously, he had murdered his father in a roadside altercation, and, in the meantime, his two sons are preparing to slaughter one another on the battlefield. He will die serene and wise at a ripe old age! The women in his family too will suffer their ignoble deaths; sadly though, and by the times' doctrines and standards, their suicides will bring them neither peace nor redemption. Still, he will die serene and wise at a ripe old age! And, lest such ironic, if not absurd, twists of fate be not enough to satisfy our hunger for the agonizingly overdramatic, the story of Thebes and its wretched ruling clan is riddled with complicated but oh so predictable political intrigues, familial feuds and psychological torments.

Is it that much of a stretch of one's sensibilities, aesthetic and otherwise, to suggest that at least one component of the classical Athenian response to the Oedipal scenario might be in line with what the Italian composers of *opera buffa* and the American screenwriters of soaps and sitcoms have sought or triggered in their audiences? As much as each of these styles belongs to its particular surround and as much as each has acquired its particular place in the West's history of cultural production, the thread of excitement and catharsis links them all in a series that runs counter to our current cultural siftings of the proper and everlastingly artistic from the trite and the mundane. Worth noting here is the fact that, had such siftings been dominant at the time, they would have no doubt heaped, and ruthlessly so, both tragedy and opera under the same heading of the common and boisterously distracting. In the meantime, much has complicated our standards and perceptions: historical revisions, national heritages, intellectual and/or artistic pride and territoriality, and, lest we forget, financial returns.

Tragedy

As much as the Oedipus with whom we are most familiar is the one fixed by Sophocles, the character's life extends far beyond the tragedy with which it has become marked. Homer (*The Iliad*, Book IV and *The Odyssey*, Book XI), Aeschylus (*Seven Against Thebes*), and Euripides (*The Phoenician Women*) had already treated of man and destiny. Since, Seneca, Corneille, Hofmannsthal, Péladan, Gide, Eliot, Cocteau, Stravinsky, el-Hakim and Pasolini are but a few of the signatures borne by the reworkings of story and theme. As the reiterations multiply, no matter the era, genre or medium, what we have come to identify and value the most are their distinct variations in recasting dramatically, politically and psychologically the fate with which we all have been presumably doomed. Whether tragic, banal, satirical, joyous or prudent, the story's components remain more or less the same. What differs, what gives them their qualities as tragic, banal, satirical or what not, are the ways in which they are woven, the distances and juxtapositions they inhabit, the relations they endure and produce, and, in turn, the relations they provoke for their audiences to endure and produce.

Lest we assume that it is only we that are familiar with the plot and its details, that it is only we for whom the production has come to eclipse 'the product', let us not forget that the tragedy's first audience was well acquainted with the myth and its major detours, partly through its cultural surround, which included the above-mentioned pre-Sophoclean sources, and partly through Sophocles himself. *Antigone*, as the last instalment of the three Theban tragedies and the thematic conclusion to the accursed family's travails, was the first to be conceived and executed (in 441 BCE). By the time *Oedipus Rex* and *Oedipus at Colonus* were produced (in approximately 426 BCE and 405 BCE, respectively), the Athenian theatre-goers were already well apprised of history and fate. To borrow from Aristotle his *Poetics* terminology, Antigone's dénouement, her change in fortune, was possible only in light of her complication, i.e. in light of her family's story in its entirety up until the point at which the play that bears her name begins to unfold; *Antigone*'s complication became the source and raw material upon which Sophocles could draw for his two remaining plays' dénouement.[73]

Aristotle is instructive on a point that is much more crucial for the current discussion. As he saw it, tragedy's principal components (plot, characters, thought, spectacle, etc.) are deployed to stage not the thing that has happened, for that is the task and function of the historian, but the thing that might happen or might have happened (*Poetics*, 1451a/35–1451b/5). Tragedy for the Greek philosopher is not a representation but a creation; its merit lies not in its ability to depict an actual event or produce an accurate document, but in its arrangement and manipulation of mostly fictional events. For the Athenian philosopher, tragedian, and theatre-goer alike, the representational quality of the Sophoclean plays, the extent to which they may or may not tell a factual story, is no more relevant than the representational quality of a *Tosca* or a *Figaro,* of an *I Love Lucy* or a *Law and Order* for their respective creators and audiences. Though not always explicit, the preliminary disclaimer that what is about to unfold does not depict actual characters and events but is a figment of its author's imagination is not any the less valid. The question as to whether the works telling of Antigone, Tosca and Lucy are equal in artistic merit belongs to an altogether different discussion. Key here is the fact that the mechanisms by which all three storylines operate and the uses to which they are put are less foreign to one another than initially assumed.

Aristotle went on to argue that tragedy's audience is treated to an experience of emotional stimulation rather than historical education. While in many respects unavoidably imitative, tragedy's highest value and indeed pleasure lie in its ability to occasion the excitement and catharsis of its audience's fear and pity (*Poetics*, 1449b/25 and 1452b/30). Firmly planted in his culture, Aristotle was drawing on the Athenian understanding of tragedy as Dionysian. The domain of the god of wine and ecstasy ran the gamut from orgy to performance; intoxication was his means, purgation was his goal. The philosopher was also echoing the dictates of a Hippocratic culture that understood illness as excess in the humours and treatment as their purgation. The modern day echoes to such an outlook are not limited to Nietzsche and Nietzscheans such as Deleuze and Guattari. Indeed, Freud too will trail closely tragedy's Athenian dynamic, as he will come to identify pleasure's basic principle in terms of an economic discharge of tension rather than a hedonistic consumption of object. Indeed, for Freud, the 'pleasure' of the libidinal drive consists in its charge being bound to, intensified by and subsequently cathected through its object much as, for Aristotle, an audience's 'pleasure' rests on its fearful and/or pitiful tremor being caught up in, heightened by and subsequently released through the drama it witnesses on the stage.

An Acropolis, a La Scala and a Hollywood are much less the stagings of truth and morality and much more the sites of Dionysian manipulation, transformation and release. The unconscious too is such a site; we have come to know its productions under the headings of dreams, slips and phantasies. Such productions point to the so-called truth of their subject only insofar as they illustrate the latter's individual strategies of pleasure or, if you will, qualities as writer, director and producer. When presented with such stagings, the threads we as clinicians are most interested in picking up and following lead us not to their historical or ethical worth (Are they true? Are they morally acceptable?) Rather, it is the unconscious processes and investments by which they have been produced and the ones which they in turn may produce that form the bulk of the analytic material.

I hold this observation to be perfectly in line with the classic Freudian appreciation and use of a dream's imagery for instance, an imagery that is much less a representation or an account of a truth as it is the product of an unconscious mise en scène, the dream-work, that is itself the focus and concern of the clinical inquiry. Indeed, and once he thought he had established the universality of incest and parricide, once, in other words, he had identified what he considered to be the inevitable components of primary phantasy, Freud was much more invested in the set of particular ways in which an analysand weaves, structures and negotiates the components than in their (dare one say it?) quotidian content. The sense of newness, discovery and individuality that psychoanalysis brings its participants is hardly in their investment in what has become a joke of a myth ('Doctor, please tell me something I have not already heard, read or been warned you would say!') The sense of newness, discovery and individuality lies in uncovering the dramatic style each analysand adopts in staging the myth, in his or her poetic scriptwriting and directorial techniques, in his or her idiosyncratic modes of excitement and catharsis, in the grounds upon which these modes are erected and the purposes they are made to serve. Again, it is the unconscious as a process, rather than an account, of desire that is of the utmost priority here. Of the myth and its tragic representation very little is left of analytic import, at least as the myth of origin whose repercussions are necessarily and exclusively tragic.

Twist

Though reverential, Freud's investment in the Sophoclean script as a founding principle of psychological activity is not without its ironies. The analyst understood the myth as a representation and, in so doing, broke his own golden rule of never mistaking manifest content for latent thought or symptom for process. Much more significantly, though, Freud thought he had apprehended Oedipus on the street, in the bedroom and on the couch. In doing so, he demythologized and made common that which he had spent an entire life revering. And by making the myth common, he found himself as implicated in its dynamic as his next-door neighbour, and in ways that may not have been entirely explicit for him.

Indeed, and by solving the Sphinx's riddle, Oedipus had precipitated not only his access to the Theban throne but his subsequent destitution as well. Perhaps the solver of psychological riddles had detected in his hero's downfall what lay in wait for him should he too speak the truth of desire. Perhaps this, among all the other by now familiar reasons, would shed yet a different light on why the young Freud, so eager to prove his legitimacy and originality, did not press the Oedipal issue as much as he might otherwise have with his mentor and sounding board. One would expect that the radical discovery of incest and parricide as universal psychological bedrock would have merited more than its three measly references in a Freud–Fliess correspondence that had lasted an additional 7 years beyond the initial mention.[74] This, among yet other equally familiar reasons, would shed further light on why Freud never committed himself to a comprehensive account of the myth's dynamics and echoes. Instead, he offered but a smattering of observations and hypotheses hinting at his insights while sparing himself the fate of his accursed hero and model.

Such explanation and light cannot but be analytically hypothetical in nature. They treat much less of Freud's conscious processes as they do of the unrecognized and hence unresolved inhibitions his Oedipal axioms could not but have produced. For his part and to his credit, Freud could not have been any more consistent: he believed his hero's entanglement in an exhausting and yet unavoidable circle of causes and effects to be the fate of one and all. One can only begin to imagine the frustration, if not the fear, of a researcher caught in the vice-like grip of a truth he so desperately needed to speak but whose logic dictated that its utterance be the ground for silence and its sight the ground for blindness. It is hence no surprise that, with time, Freud's Oedipal identifications found refuge in and became the symptoms of yet another mythological entanglement. While speaking Oedipus, the psychoanalyst began to live the logic of a Sisyphus, barely glimpsing the open landscape of relief only to have to wearily give it up and descend the slopes of blindness he had just scaled, and begin all over again. Caught in the logic of such hopeless repetition, no wonder his analysis had become interminable. Meanwhile, and yet again, Freud's re-enactment of this second myth illustrates, and in the strictest of psychoanalytic ways, the extent to which our conscious experiences of fate and punishment are often grounded in covert but no less potent choice and collusion.

On the other hand, Freud could not have been any more inconsistent for having remained silent about a presumably blinding truth while advocating speech as the principal instrument of insight. There is nothing triumphal about such an observation for Freud's was not a logical inconsistency, let alone a clinical hypocrisy. Freud's was the deep-seated psychological ambivalence one lives through and witnesses daily, on the couch, in the bedroom and on the street. What the ambivalence does however is betray the sway of not a single myth but that of a host of Olympian characters crowded inside a Pandora's box from which the psychoanalyst falsely hoped he could retrieve only those scripts he had deemed useful. Alongside an Oedipus, a Dionysus and a Sisyphus, one can also find an Adonis born out of incest but suffering none of the trials of an Antigone, or a Thamyris blinded by the Muses for his mortal vanity rather than for his poetic blunders or even a Nemesis countering the careless and haphazard fortunes bestowed by a Tyche. The reference to Nemesis here is not to her modern day collapsing onto the logic of opposition and enmity but to her original place in the classic Greek lexicon as a nymph-goddess of redress symbolized by the wheel of transformation from peak to pit, and back again.

While swearing allegiance to some of the gods, demi-gods and *dramatis personae* of ancient Athens, Freud had in fact refused to acknowledge and suffer his idols as multiple, impetuous and violent. To be fair to Freud, again, his was not a singular or idiosyncratic betrayal. We are all invariably confronted with an immense and seemingly infinite network of meanings and words, characters and dynamics, that we hastily reduce to what we, at any given point in time, find manageable and/or useful. We devise systems of reference along whose axes we can begin to pin a sense and a service. We select; we bracket; we prioritize; we abstract; we interpret. Faced with the other alternative, the one that is all too keen to deploy the multiplicity of meanings and values as a justification for upholding the futility of any and all intervention, Freud's often seems quite a responsible route for us to take.

Hubris

Regardless, the generally held view, the one that psychoanalysis has recapitulated but not yet fully explored, is that the kernel of the Sophoclean script treats of a three-sided violation: Oedipus was doomed as much for his attempt at defying the Delphic oracle as he was for his parricide and incest. The two latter crimes were of a common quality to the classical Athenian mind, at least in the context of a mytho-theology that was replete with incidences of what we nowadays might consider as even more obscene and absurd passions and events. This, of course, would not have made the king's treatment of his parents any the less heinous, but it would have rendered it in paler colours in comparison with his even more sinister and intolerable defiance as a mere mortal. His refusal to submit to the dictates of the higher deities, his though well-intentioned but not any the less desperate and misguided wish for the fallibility of their oracles, which is to say his willed ignorance of these oracles' influence and authority, and, in the process, his attempt to arrogate as his own their powers and privileges, his, in other words, refusal to recognize and abide by his station as a flawed and powerless human in an otherwise rigidly organized cast system is what ultimately cost him his royal privilege.

Two aspects of the example of Antigone are instructive on this point: the first is political and the second psychological. Her father's daughter, Antigone thought that she too could circumvent the laws of the state in favour of a heavenly commandment to which she declared herself subject. To her mind, she also became that commandment's enforcer, protector and agent. Initially its tool, she subtly but steadily transformed herself into its master; subject to its authority, she became its authoritative subject. Following in her footsteps, many of *Antigone*'s modern readers have heard in her the voice of a conscience that is righteous, a conscience that will be seduced neither by the little pleasures of the everyday nor by a rationality that is ostensibly nothing more than a pretext or a justification after the fact. However, and for most of her Athenian audiences, Antigone, like her father, would have probably remained the blasphemous pretender to a seat at the Olympian high table; her hubris would have been a trigger for her audience's indignation, dismissal and pity. Quite likely, her death would have been seen as the product of a misplaced, disgraceful and even laughable sense of allegiance rather than a lofty sacrifice since, and to the mind of her contemporaries, suicide was cowardly and self-indulgent and she was but a woman, foolhardy, irrational and unenviable. On the other hand, Creon's final torment at his loss of honour and family may very well have been the play's climactic moment and the worthiest of its audience's compassion and sympathy.

The other aspect to Antigone's scenario worth noting here is her psychological structure which, sadly, has eluded much of the current analysis of the Theban trilogy. Let us pause for a moment and consider the following: Antigone is the product of incest; her father was a murderer and her mother committed suicide; her two brothers failed utterly at containing their sibling rivalries; they in fact ended up killing each other on the battlefield. Antigone has also spent much of her adult life in exile ministering to her blind and dishonoured father and half-brother, a man toward whom she must have felt some hint of revulsion. Would it be too much of a stretch to suggest that, as one might say these days, she has 'baggage'? Would it be even remotely possible that, as someone who has lived in the midst of, and been shaped by, so much unmitigated violence and destruction, Antigone could only come to act on her aggression and on her envy toward Creon as the only family member who was not manifestly implicated by the oracles and their damned and damning prophecies? She is carried away by her rage at her (grand) uncle; she will trigger a chain of events that will leave him waiting for his death, weak, sexless and childless. She will effectively castrate him. True to her name, Antigone is not only the one without progeny; she is the woman who will arrogate for herself the manly power to bring a family's entire patriarchal lineage to its end. She will come to embody that vision of femininity men have reviled and women have fought against.

It seems to me that Antigone is deserving of something other than the ruthless dismissal she must have suffered at the hands of her Athenian audiences or the abstract elaborations on psyche and righteousness she has come to endure from her modern readers. If these latter are on the right track then it would be quite the comic feat of justice if, two and a half millennia from now, their psychologies and politics were to be filtered through whatever traces will have survived of *Beaches* or *Days of Our Lives.*

Identification

It is not a coincidence that psychoanalysis aims not to remove the incestuous and the murderous but to mitigate the will to ignorance that surrounds them, that, in other words, its clinical claim, at its humblest and, paradoxically, at its strongest, is not to eradicate but to transform. However, and whereas the practice has grown to mime in the clinical manifestations of the Oedipal flight from Corinth something other than the escapist, and whereas its response to such adaptations has far surpassed the simplistic charge of resistance or defensiveness, the classical Athenian sensibility could not or would not have afforded such futile attempts at flight anything other than pity. The logic of identification so dear to the modern readers of the Theban tragedies as allegories of a basic human condition ('Aren't we all oh so incestuous and parricidal!') would have been countered with an equally potent but nowadays overlooked logic of distance and dis-identification ('Look at the arrogant and miserable fool who tries to flee the inviolable dictates of the gods!'), a logic that is grounded in yet another identificatory move that has more to do with the audience than with the spectacle.

Let us not ignore the fact that both the play and the psychological responses it is designed to elicit are inscribed in the context of the performance as a collective event rife with its own set of multiple and conflicted identificatory dynamics. Indeed, and as much as the relational vectors may be trafficking between the audience and the characters on the stage, an equally critical set of psychological and affective scenarios are at work off that stage, binding the theatre-goers and imbuing them with the sense of a cohesive group identity that will in turn redirect, reinforce or even reproduce the dynamics of its individual members as anti-Oedipal and/or non-Oedipal in matters of incest, parricide and, most importantly, defiance of the Olympian gods and their rules. These are indeed the most law-abiding of anti-Oedipal audiences; their experiences and responses expose the exclusionary fallacy that underlies any simplistic bifurcation, whether Deleuzo-Guattarian or Freudian.

The identifications in such a context are always multiple and conflicted. As the audience sees in Oedipus a horrible script that may very well turn out to be its own, it simultaneously recognizes in him that which it itself is not. Though powerful, the king is physically lame; though once a saviour, he is now a curse; before his audience, he stands as simultaneously hero and anti-hero, ally and enemy. Ultimately, the vertical identification with the leader Freud had articulated in his work on group psychology cannot but be co-extensive with its negative and/or mirror image: the dis-identification with the rebel, renegade or lawbreaker who has mistaken him or her self for a leader and who may, elsewhere or otherwise, eventually become one (Figure 4). In the meantime, both dynamics reinforce what for the group is at the core of its constitution as homogeneity rather than a disparate collectivity. We shall soon see how such obedience and homogeneity help reconfigure the play as much more comically moralistic than tragic.

To reduce the aesthetic interaction between audience and performance to a logic of discrete identification ('this or that character is the one to hold

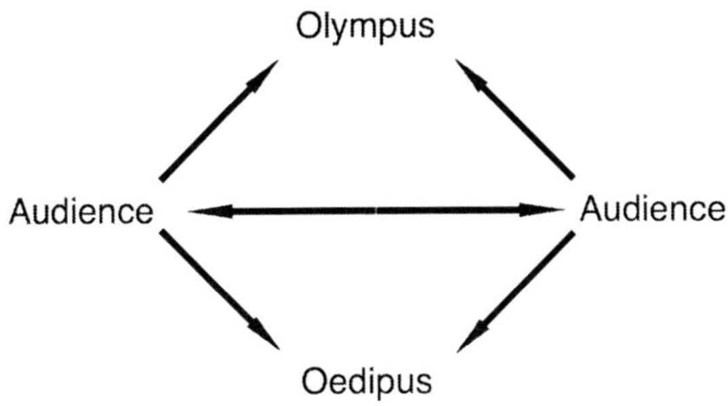

FIGURE 4

as the object of one's truth, esteem or censure'), and to organize around such a logic a singular psychological structure which presumably we must all either obey or defy strikes me as the farthest one could move from the spirit of the Freudian enterprise. Much like in a dream, the staging of the Sophoclean characters' trials and adventures operates as the manifest outcome of a series of displacements, condensations and revisions that are inevitably layered and multiple. Much like in a dream, and with Freud, we have also learned that such a staging is never fixed in meaning and purpose, that, depending on its context, every retelling of the series of images and impressions elicits its own set of associations and hence offers its own significance and exerts its own impact. Furthermore, we have learned that our unconscious identifications are never limited to this or that of the dream's components but to the totality of its characters and dynamics. We may stage a manifest division of labour among the characters, allocating our anxieties to some, our desires to others, and our aggressions to others still; analytically, however, we appreciate that such allocations are temporary and instrumental. However much we may wish them not to be so, the anxieties, desires and aggressions are not any the less ours.

Most crucial in the audience's play of identifications is hence the totality of the Sophoclean staging as object of recognition and valuation. It is that staging that recreates the world in a way that the audience appreciates; and that is why that audience will in turn appreciate it as its voice and reflection (Figure 5). That is also why we may prefer the staging of a Sophocles, a Cocteau or a Pasolini to that of a Péladan, a Seneca or a Gide. While these dramatists have treated of the same story, each has cast it according to a particular technique and sensibility with which we may or may not identify. This is also why, clinically, we invite an analysand to 'identify' not with the person of the analyst as the presumably healthy character on the stage of the treatment but with analysis as a style, a perspective and a sensibility.

Audience ← Sophocles → Audience

Figure 5

In staging father and daughter the way he did, was Sophocles the first diagnostician of a delusional disorder of a grandiose type? Perhaps our colleagues the modern day compilers of psychiatric profiles and categories have unwittingly deployed the dramatist as source and inspiration? No matter, since most revealing at this point is the polyvalence that marks Greek tragedy as a distinctive dramatic art. Nemesis and her wheel have struck again. She carries the adult Oedipus from heir to a throne to lame wanderer, to king, to outcast, to sacred figure. She submits his Thebes to routine cycles of prosperity and pestilence. All the while, she sways her audience between the two poles of fear and pity. At its core, the logic of Nemesis disobeys the laws of authenticity that segregate what is genuine and true from what is a distraction or a cover; with it, neither the crying nor the laughter is the primary or authentic response; and neither is a cover or a defence for the other. They are synchronic and co-constitutive. 'I laughed, I cried.'

In keeping with Nemesis and her wheel, and alongside Aristotelian fear and pity, we might want to add to the circumference of audience responses and experiences horror, contempt, Schadenfreude, concern, relief – comic or otherwise – love, despair, triumph, frustration, wonder, exasperation, bewilderment; in fact, we might want to add as many passions as there are points to that circumference (Figure 6). In so doing, we appreciate that as much as libido is an inherently polyvalent force whose varied components have been intertwined in ways specific to an individual's temperament and history, so too is the response to its representation, on the stage, on the page or in the dream. Overdetermination as a marker of the psyche and its operations is not any the more compelling in matters sexual than in matters representational and Oedipus need not be an exception to its rule. Put differently, the insistence that the Theban plays ought to be nothing but painful tragedies makes as little analytic sense, whether psycho or schizo, as the insistence that sexuality ought to be nothing but a dutiful procreation.

Laughter

Might there then be a place for laughter, in however many shades and nuances, in such a context? Structurally and culturally, the laughter is not only viable and predictable, it is in fact necessary; without it, the Nemetic

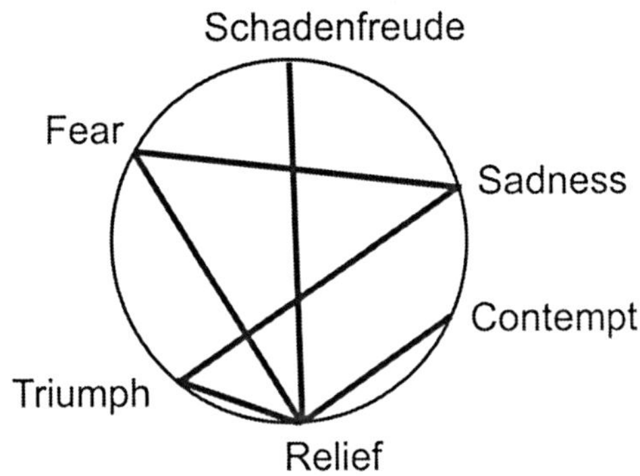

Figure 6

wheel would be shattered and its parts dispersed. It really does not require that much of a leap in one's imagination to register the waves of farcical, humorous, sadistic or satirical chuckles sweeping across the Sophoclean audience. Look out for the noble and upright king who, because of his pierced ankles, has to hobble his way across the stage. Make sure not to miss our hero's hyperboles for everything about his words and deeds is in line with the basic structure of humour as exaggerated non-sense. Note the sympathy you feel for him as he heaps his misdeeds and confusions one upon the other, à la Lucy Ricardo, desperate for the clear-minded and practical interventions of a Creon, his Ricky.[75] Keep track of our hero's familial lines as they progressively blur beyond recognition: his children are his siblings; his brother-in-law is his uncle; his daughter will soon plan to marry the man who is both his nephew and cousin. Many of Jerry Springer's most outlandish of scenarios could only dream of such twists and complications. Last but not least, do not overlook Jocasta, Antigone and Euridyce's final suicidal gestures, sacrificial and redemptive only from the point of view of a modernity that has been thoroughly Christianized; to their original audiences, which, incidentally, were almost exclusively male, they remained pitiable and laughable.

Was the classical Athenian theatre-goer any more resistant to the temptations of laughter and hooting than the modern day viewer of television talk shows and situation comedies? Was he any blinder to the absurdly comedic, was he any more aesthetically refined, any more sensitive, any nobler, any less moralistic, any less adolescent? Hardly. Are we then disavowing our own insensitivity and adolescence and setting ourselves up as the nobler ones by recasting the Athenian drama and distilling it down to what we have conveniently declared as its purest and loftiest? To me, that would be more likely.

The widely held view that, properly remounted, any tragic play can be easily transformed into a comedy, a farce even, is not the position I wish to advance here. Sophocles did not lie in wait for P. D. Q. Bach's *Oedipus Tex* to compliment his drama; nor did he produce a holographic trinket that changes its reflection depending on the perspective from which it is seen. His text is not a sophomoric 'now it's a rabbit, now it's an old woman' experiment in the psychology of perception; nor is it a blank screen upon which one simply projects the existential torments of one's day. Rather, the play and its text are invariably constituted by and constitutive of a gamut of affects and responses that far surpass the logics of not only the singularity of tragedy but of the duality and ambivalence of tragicomedy as well. In this respect, Beckett could not have paid the Greek dramatist a better tribute than through a short play (*Act Without Words I*) whose solo character clownishly, sadly, desperately, doggedly, childishly, and earnestly 'reflects' on a situation into which he finds himself thrown, literally, repeatedly. He makes us laugh, with him, at him and for him; we identify with the futility of his predicament; we smirk at his awkward reach for simple props he does not know how to employ; we relish in his ponderous poses as we also desperately wish we could lend him a helping hand. The ingenuity of his creator lies in having made him clown, hero, dullard and reflection all at the same time; and it is this ingenuity that we value.

To return to our original script, two considerations are worth noting here, the one cultural and the other religious. Each adds further to the project of appreciating the Sophoclean scenario as but a node in a network that extends beyond the confines of the singular and/or individualistic. Each also expands the scenario's gamut of experiences and responses. Tragedy in the Athens of Sophocles was performed as a component of the Greater Dionysia. The festive cycle was designed and executed as a dynamic unity of which comedy was an integral part. Its audience often knew what to expect in terms of the plot and characters within any particular play; it also knew that its participation in the festival was tantamount to a ride on an emotional roller coaster of tears and laughter, sorrow and joy, pity and levity, and everything in between; t treated such a ride as a continuum rather than an artificial concatenation of discrete and contradictory affects. Along with the dramatists and performers of its day, this audience understood fully well that each moment and each affect was necessary and indeed special, but not especially so.

Parallel is the religious register under which the dramatic festival was conceived and executed. The Greater Dionysia was mounted yearly in the springtime as a celebration of and a tribute to the god of rebirth and fertility. The festival's affective richness and elasticity echo a long-standing ritual of ecstasy and excess familiar to many of the region's cultures and across many of its histories. As far back as the fourteenth century BCE. the tears of the gods were recognized as not only products of grief but as instruments of satiety, intoxication even. Flemming Friis Hvidberg invokes certain Canaanite tablets that tell of the goddess Anat's drinking of tears like wine upon hearing the news of the death of her brother Ba'al and argues that this far from simple connection between crying and intoxication, sadness and joy, extended to the bereaved goddess's worshipers (*Weeping and Laughter*, 15–56). As Tom Lutz has since described it, a springtime ritual among the Canaanites saw the members of an entire tribe

> remove themselves to the desert and begin to slowly moan and cry, moving from whimpering to weeping to wailing and then, over the course of several days, to frenzied hysterics and finally to laughing exhilaration before dissolving into giggles and resuming everyday life. (*Crying*, 33–34)

In such a context, and as Lutz points out, tears and laughter combine not as opposites but as way stations on a continuum of emotions whose expression is a source of both individual pleasure and social cohesion (34). As Lutz traces the echoes of this continuum across various cultures in the Old Testament, I would suggest that they find their way into the drama modernity has marked as one of that geography's highest moments of cultural achievements and that we have since reworked and censored that moment in the manner of a collective secondary revision intelligible to us only as a lofty tragedy forever burdened by virtually all the other dramatic styles as its supposedly illegitimate and derivative cousins.

Revision

As for the effects of such a revision, Freud has already argued in *Totem and Taboo* that they are not exclusive to the dream-work; they are in fact evidenced in any realm of thought that requires unity and intelligibility as markers of its systematic aspirations. Freud writes that

> [t]he secondary revision of the product of the dream-work is an admirable example of the nature and pretensions of a system. There is an intellectual function in us which demands unity, connection and intelligibility from any material, whether of perception or thought, that comes within its grasp; and if, as a result of special circumstances, it is unable to

> establish a true connection, it does not hesitate to fabricate a false one . . . [A] system is best characterized by the fact that at least two reasons can be discovered for each of its products: a reason based upon the premises of the system (a reason, then, which may be delusional) and a concealed reason, which we must judge to be the truly operative and the real one. (*Totem and Taboo*, 154)

Unwittingly, Freud may very well have been predicting and facilitating the course of the criticism the intellectual function of his own apparatus was soon to suffer. Indeed, his appraisal of a system's need for unity and intelligibility applies equally to metapsychology as it does to the structures of which it speaks. The psychoanalyst's view stands here in stark opposition to Ockham's razor as the principle of theoretical parsimony that has dominated much of the West's scientific inquiry and the aesthetic standards of its formulations from the early Renaissance onwards. Interestingly enough, psychoanalysis too has often found itself loath to resist such a principle. No matter its internal struggles and divisions, the discipline has invariably sought to extract from the richness of its subject matter as basic and as universal a set of dynamics and categories as it possibly could. For Freud, it was the unconscious as a process that negotiates the pressures of the libido; for Klein, envy and gratitude provided the major keys to the psyche's workings and possible transformations; for Lacan, registers and mathemes were the code words by which the practice of the cure may be assessed and validated; and the list goes on.

Whether axiomatic or real, explicit or concealed, I would like to suggest that one of the main motivating factors, or 'reasons' as Freud wishes them to be, behind such a pursuit of systematic unity and simplicity is the discipline's long-standing thirst for recognition as a member in our modern day version of the Greek Pantheon: Science. The price for such recognition cannot be overestimated. Much like the dramatic storm around which it has organized its practice and much like the blind hero around whom it has mounted its own clinical and intellectual storm, psychoanalysis has remained largely blind to the material and psychological paucity of its understanding of the psyche and, by extension, of sexuality, as tragically Oedipal and nothing but. Psychoanalysis persists in its refusal to acknowledge that for it to do justice to the panoply of human passions it must recognize itself, as both a method and a community, as subject to them. Instead, it often discourses on sexuality in the most un-seductive of styles and on desire in the most un-desirous. It, after all, is a Science. Humour it virtually ignores; humility, it seems, it has yet to discover; auto-irony it finds intolerable.

Sadly, it stands alone as did Antigone, tragic in her certitude but no less comedic in her zeal.

This, fortunately, is not the fate to which psychoanalysis must be doomed. While the abundance of its caricatures in the popular mind is a symptom of hostility and defensiveness, it is also a sign of the discipline's own intensely disavowed and split off comedic power. As I see it, the collective and clinical task at this point is to reintegrate that power, not as aim but as tool. To do so would involve the recognition that laughter is a moment in the analytic process that is not always reducible to either a defence against an intolerable anxiety or a sadistic judgement regarding an unacceptable situation. The bodily reverberation of laughter is at times the instantiation of a mood and an experience that have long given up on the convenient splits between right and wrong, victim and culprit. This reverberation is the symptom of neither Oedipal resolution nor anti-Oedipal mockery.

Redemption

There is yet another set of reasons operative in the psychoanalytic attempt at unity and intelligibility, one that lies as much on the side of the analysand in search of a 'cure' as it does with the one administering it. In spite of all his blunders and sufferings, Oedipus the tragic and pained figure is also the ultimate metaphor of hope and redemption. While ignominy and despair rule all around, we see him in his final days in *Oedipus at Colonus* convinced in his wisdom and secure in his fate; his burial ground will be declared sacred and inaccessible to mere mortals. As a secularized re-staging of that other scene of sacrifice and revelation whose image of the cross has gripped much of the West for the past 2 millennia, myth and theme combine to produce in their modern day subscriber a more than adequate ground for the investment and the gain. The contemporary Oedipal may not be able to undo their familial and psychological pasts; they may not be able to circumvent their bodily predicaments; and they certainly may not be able to protect their loved ones from their own ill-fated errors. These Oedipal may, however, reframe and refunction their histories and limits in such a way as to guarantee for themselves a peace, if not a sacredness, that will justify the pain of their misery and destitution as a right of passage. They are no longer the accursed many; they are the courageous few that have crossed their deserts, borne their crosses and transcended their births.

Freud's words of warning to his prospective analysands may function as a level-headed and perhaps even humble and humbling admonition regarding psychoanalysis as a painful and lengthy process that carries with it hardly any guarantee of success. However, Freud's words also convey the challenge, the dare and perhaps even the plea to sacrifice one's dearest, traverse one's harshest and confront one's deepest, to, and in line with his abundant images of conquest and progress, remain standing where many before have fallen. Such challenge, dare and plea are welcomed at least partly because through them one may now trace one's sufferings across the ages to that noble scene of recovery. How many would want to forgo the opportunity for such lineage and identification? How many would opt for a less mystifying extraction? At this point, 'as few' and 'as many' stand an equal chance of being the correct answer.

Nemesis

Finally, and in what could only be described as a brilliant move of intellectual foresight, if not sabotage, Freud's remarks in the above *Totem and Taboo* passage prescribe a similar diagnosis to the systems from which his detractors will subsequently come to launch their own clinical and/or metapsychological missives. At this stage, I do not hold my own comments to be immune to such a predicament. I do, however, hold that any theory of the unconscious as an inherently multiple and disorganizing process must itself tolerate multiplication and disorganization.

In the meantime, and as a Nemetic gesture, I would like to offer a return to the period Jacob Burckhardt treats, a period that in turn had committed itself to a recapitulation and re-enlivenment of the best antiquity had bequeathed it. In the Florence of the 1590s, a group of literati known as the Camerata di Bardi had set for itself the task of resurrecting on the stage, and in as accurate a way as it knew how, the myths and tragedies of ancient Athens. For this, the Camerata relied mostly on the commentaries and criticisms it had uncovered in the texts of earlier tragedians and philosophers. Consistent among these was the reference to music as an integral component of staging and performance. Having at their disposal nothing but a handful of ancient musical scores they could not yet decipher, the members of the Camerata sought to combine words and music in ways that best suited their dramatic purposes and sensibilities. With the recitative, 'drama in music' was born and, but a few years later, Claudio Monteverdi emerged as the clearly identifiable first in a long tradition of opera composers.

In providing a historical and cultural link between two of the West's richest artistic epochs (classical Athens and Modern Europe), the fact of the Florentine Camerata witnesses how the latter has often obfuscated a crucial ingredient of the former. At its root, the operatic project did not deny itself a healthy dose of levity nor did it consider itself superior to the requirements of mass entertainment. Indeed, Giovanni de' Bardi, the leader of the Camerata, was renowned for his flamboyant stagings replete with lavish settings, sumptuous costumes and extravagant floral arrangements. Often, at least as far as Bardi was concerned, the point to such excess was to render tragedy even more lush and magnificent than comedy itself (*Della tragedia*, 133). Bardi was frequently called upon when his rivals and contemporaries, such as Michelangelo Buonarroti il Giovane, would simply not rise to the challenge of exaggeration. While the recent upsurge in multi-mediatic productions of classic operatic works attempts to revitalize the art and free it from the constraints of the burdensome and earnest Hochkultur of the nineteenth century, Florence and its neighbour Venice had already caught on to opera's entertainment effect by the late 1600s. Indeed, and within 50 years of the art's inception, dozens of opera houses had sprung across the northern Italian landscape where, true to Bardi's spirit, productions often featured cloud machines, shipwrecks, volcanoes, elephants and bears regardless of plot and storyline.

The point to all of this is that the dominant psychoanalytic rendering of Oedipus as nothing but an austere and solemn tragedy is hardly without its historical biases. That in his interpretation Freud was fixed to the cultural determinants of his day is understandable, if not predictable. That, over a century later, psychoanalysis ought to remain uncritically faithful to such an interpretation, at the expense of all past or future others, is not. That schizoanalysis should buy into the claim that such an interpretation is the only one to undermine and dismantle and that once such a manoeuvre has been accomplished nothing much will be left of Oedipus is even less understandable.

Chapter Six

Cixous: the unseen seen

To speak of laughter and its reverberations as I began to in the previous chapter is to revisit the relationship between body and word in the analytic situation and to recast it in terms that invoke something other than priority, whether of word or experience or even of the power of a word or a specific kind of experience. Such a priority has been invariably set up in the service of a process of identification with or against a law, a myth or indeed biology. The unconscious as a form of thought unsettles the workings of a rationality ossified around static and mutually exclusive disjunctions; ditto for Nemesis as she unravels the Oedipus that has been reproduced by classical psychoanalysis and rebelled against by the schizoanalytic project; as for biology, I will try and show in the following pages that it is much too subtle to be subsumed under any single overarching category of truth or harnessed in the service of a single logic of identification.

On this score, Deleuze once invited us to think identity and sameness not as the logical ground from which difference ensues but as 'the manifest content' of 'a condensation of coexistences and a simultaneity of events' (*The Logic of Sense*, 262). Though the product of a deep disparity, this identity does not speak of either normative copies, or melancholic and hence failed duplicates, or even of cheap and irrelevant imitations. Deleuze's classic Freudian terminology here need neither confuse nor mislead us. As manifest content, identity is not the mere distortion of a latent and disconcerting but ostensibly much truer and more primal difference. Deleuze's psychoanalytic echo is not to that of the Freud of 1899 whose schema in *The Interpretation of Dreams* designates the latent thought as primary at the expense of all the other components of a dream. Deleuze's echo is to the Freud of 1925 who, in a footnote to his most favoured text, identified the productive work of condensation, displacement, symbolization and revision as the essence of dreaming and the explanation of its differentiating and individualizing nature.[76] Deleuze's echo is to the ever-shifting constellation of the three indispensable elements of the dream: latent thought, manifest content and dream work. Here, the order of participation, the fixity of distribution and the determination of hierarchy are all rendered impossible. Following in the footsteps of Nietzsche, Deleuze articulates an identity that is highlighted not only as a produced and hence potentially dispensable effect instead of a fixed category, but also as a product that may or may not be re-inscribed in a circuit of differences leading to future products and effects.

I would like to carry this echo yet another step further and invoke the recent challenge of the British psychoanalytic thinker Adam Phillips. Phillips recounts Kafka's parable of the leopards whose regular storming of the temple is subsequently interpreted by the believers as a necessary part of their religious ceremony (*Terrors and Experts*, 67–71). Phillips argues for a parallel scenario concerning the presence and valence of dreams in the analytic process: 'psychoanalysis is a conceptual apparatus that invites the leopards into the temple, and makes them integral to the ceremony' (73). While their initial appearance in the analytic setting may have been coincidental, dreams seem to have overtaken the entire process as its foundation and primary mode of operation. Regardless of whether or not I agree with his position, there is something refreshingly machinic to the strategy Phillips adopts; leaning against the contributions of such pillars as Massud Khan and Jean-Bertrand Pontalis, he directs his query much less toward the meanings of dreams and more so toward their contexts, uses and agencies. I would like to suggest that couplets such as identity/difference, or theory/practice and subject/object for that matter, and in whatever combination or order of relevance – Freudian, Deleuzian, or otherwise – may very well turn out to be nothing but the leopards that have infiltrated our current conceptual and clinical ceremonies. While some may choose to continue in the rituals as they stand, leopards et al., others are more than justified in at least contemplating the possibility of rituals sans leopards, the possibility of thinking and analysing, as Michel Foucault somewhere once put it, 'elsewhere and otherwise'.

Pinnings

I would like to return to Richard Powers' assertion that 'in evolution's beginning was not the word but the place we learned to pin the word to' (*Galatea 2.2*, 248). There is something quite unsettling about this declaration of Powers', psychoanalytically at least. As a talking cure, our practice has often slipped from focusing on the word to privileging it, and sometimes to the point of fixing it as the ground for what constitutes a human being. We have been trained to recognize language and its structures as not simply the tools by which we communicate our inner realities but as the building blocks of our psyches, cultures and practices. While this is indeed the case, we have sadly forgotten that it is not just words that inhabit our consulting rooms, that the words are thought and uttered by bodies, and that the connections between words and bodies are ones we have just barely begun to appreciate, let alone understand. On those rare occasions when we do take stock of our materialities, we tend to relegate them to those lower strata that have not yet been spoken, and which, once spoken, would presumably either cease to have any relevance or have their impact contained and regulated. In this context, we have rendered the non-verbal as synonymous with the pre-verbal, as, in other words, the leftover or debris of a process of maturation that is obviously still in the making, and whose making the cure has set for itself as definition, challenge and aim.

For now, I would like to defer the debate over priorities and hierarchies, a debate that is also over power, territoriality and professional privilege, if not legitimacy. After all, we as analysts are confronted almost daily with the pressure to justify and prove the efficacy of our approach in an environment of speed and expediency where the latest psychoactive concoction, cognitive manoeuvre, or self-help recipe reigns supreme as lord and personal saviour. I would also like to defer the debate over timelines and precedents between soma and psyche, physiology and unconscious. If pressed, my inclination would be to reject the bias of development and succession and to argue instead for a principle of simultaneity or concurrence. More specifically, my question would not be 'Which came first, psyche or soma?' or even 'In what exact proportions do psyche and soma contribute to a particular scenario or constellation?' My question would instead be: at any given point in time, what connections obtain between the various components, and what among the investments and effects can be maintained or refunctioned? To return to the statement made by Powers, I am much more interested in the agencies, occasions and purposes of the pinnings of word to place, and vice versa. My working assumptions are that we cannot do without such pinnings, that they are multifarious, that they are a lifelong occupation if not the matter of life itself, and that, consequently, much of ossification, both psychic and somatic, occurs at those moments and in those spaces when the pinnings themselves have become ossified or have altogether ceased. To appreciate such pinnings is then to understand them in the context of the spaces from which they have emerged and to re-engage them with the perspectives through which they have been experienced.

Among such spaces and perspectives, I want to highlight here conversion hysteria and passing disability. The first is a classic, but not any the less controversial, among the psychoanalytic categories. Freud identified conversion as that mechanism by which an unresolved unconscious conflict is transposed onto the body where the symptom, be it motor or sensory, is designed to absorb that conflict's investments and in the process attempt its resolution. The pinning in this case is both economic and symbolic: economic in that the energies of the psyche are taken up by the body and symbolic in that the bodily symptom is connected to the psychic conflict in a relation of meaning and representation.[77] Note here the order of the progression: from unconscious conflict as ground, to bodily malfunction as outcome, with economic transposition and symbolic formulation as the passages from the one to the other.

The second instance of pinning I would like to take up is that of passing disability. I use the expression here to refer to those physiological characteristics, whether they are accrued through accident or heredity, that put serious limitations on an individual's abilities to participate fully in the everyday, with the proviso that, unless spoken, they remain virtually unavailable to the untrained observer. Myopia and cone dystrophy are poignant examples from the field of vision; various degrees of partial deafness and certain categories of brain injury fit the bill as well. Unlike their so-called hysterical counterparts that often revel in public display, such conditions remain largely hidden and thus allow their bearers to pass as, presumably, fully abled.

With this opposition, we have the beginnings of a structural relationship between conversion hysteria and passing disability that is quasi-specular in nature, that, in other words, reveals the one as a constitutive mirror reflection of the other:

- While the ground of hysteria is psychological and its effect physiological, the reverse is the case for the disability.
- While the pinning in both operates along symbolic and economic lines, hysteria demands a degree of public visibility while the passing disability remains for the most part unseen.
- While hysteria's dynamics are frequently unaccompanied by conscious cognition, disability rarely leaves any room for indifference.
- While hysteria's physiological impasse is subject to linguistic intervention, if not dissipation, disability's is often immune to it.

Before I proceed any further, I would like to effect a manoeuvre, a pinning, that may, or may not, run counter to the spirit of what is frequently organized under the heading of 'applied psychoanalysis'. From Freud onwards, we observe a major investment by clinicians in matters non-clinical as they apply the findings and techniques of analytic inquiry to extra-analytic phenomena: literature, history, science, war, sculpture, religion, etc. While testifying to the tremendous richness and usefulness of the psychoanalytic insight, it is striking, to me at least, how rare it is for that insight to be significantly affected, modified or influenced by the extra-analytic objects it treats. It is as if such treatments and encounters are intended to shed a light on only one of the two parties concerned (the object) while leaving the other (the insight) virtually intact, if not further confirmed in its priority and legitimacy. So, and instead of seeking comfort in having found Oedipus, the depressive position, or the objet petit a alive and well off the couch as much as on it, I would like to deploy the material that follows not as means for verifying my psychoanalytic hypotheses but as tools that will hopefully egg them on in directions they would not have pursued otherwise. I will have virtually nothing original to say about what has taken place outside the consulting room for I am neither historian nor critic; but I would like to use what has been said about that outside to shed some light on the inside.

Counting

The problematic relationship between word and place, that is to say between mind and body, is a relationship that twentieth century research in gender and sexuality has taught us is not without its biased connotations. Indeed, the word that may have been at the beginning, the word whose primacy I am putting in question here is much less a disembodied word as it is the word that belongs to the universal (read: masculine/heterosexual) body. An account of the connection between conversion and passing must therefore treat of the relationship between speech and silence, visibility and invisibility, as categories that have dominated our cultural, political, and scientific discourses on not only the masculine and the feminine, but the heterosexual and the homosexual as well. Conversion hysteria is a product of thought; it is visible, active, public; it subscribes to a logic of daylight, presence and expression; there is something quasi-melancholic (as Freud understood the term) to its persistence for it speaks little of retreat or self-effacement; it is not shy; it is masculine; it is heterosexual. Passing disability seems depressive in its reticence; it is bodily, dark; it is private to the point of silence and invisibility; it is feminine, homosexual.

My intentional realignment of the categories of hysteria and masculinity is not the mark of a so-called 'deconstruction' of the customary practices of bifurcation and allocation that have traditionally pinned the phenomenon onto the feminine and the homosexual. Rather, it is, and as will become evident later, a pointer to these practices' inherent confusion and a preliminary ground for the unseating of gender and sexual difference as the primary sites of identity and health. In order to do so, I would like to focus first on a strain in the history of artistic production that has taken up the problematic of pinning and that has accounted for, which is to say counted, the relationship between word and place, psyche and soma, perspective and figure. I would like to develop a temporary and tactical homology between this strain and some of what has been taken up and worked through in the clinical literature concerning the dynamics and dimensions of the transference.

Allow me then to introduce you to *Les deux amies*:[78] the woman on the right is Gabrielle d'Estrées, mistress of Henry IV, King of France, and the woman on the left is one of her sisters, either the duchess of Villars or the marechale of Balagny – of this we are not entirely certain. The painting belongs to the second school of Fontainebleau; its creator is unknown, and its date lies somewhere between 1594 and 1599. This work is governed by a fundamental contradiction between power and disenfranchisement: the power inherent to the display of two women in a homoerotic moment and the disenfranchisement of lesbian relations by a church whose Council of Trent had just re-codified the sacrament of marriage as a monogamous heterosexual union; the power of key women on the political stage, including Gabrielle d'Estrées herself, as well as Marguerite de Navarre, Diane de Poitiers and Catherine de Medici, and the disenfranchisement of women from political life by a revamping of the lines of succession to the French throne from which women were henceforth categorically excluded. In her brilliant study of the painting, Marie-Jo Bonnet traces this contradiction to the theatrical composition of the painting, with the edge of the bathtub delineating the stage that separates actor from spectator, the drawn curtains further emphasizing the theatrical distance, and the backdrop of another painting as the stage set to the overall scene. Bonnet suggests that such a theatricality can only point to its other as the lived and the real, that, in effect, the couple is only a representation, a copy or an imitation that cannot yet define itself fully and as subject, either sexually or politically (*Les deux amies*, 50–51).

The painting's play of dualities here leaves us at a bit of a loss precisely because it is confined to a counting to two that is inherently disjunctive and oppositional: power or disenfranchisement, representation or subject, actor or spectator, not to mention masculine or feminine, heterosexual or homosexual, licit or illicit. As much as it may be a staging that is firmly anchored in an appreciation for theatrical depth, a residue of flatness is nonetheless crucial for the painting's composition as it makes no allowance whatsoever for perspective. Painter and viewer may very well be 2 or 20 feet away from the stage or canvas, the effect of distance on composition and proportion would hardly be relevant. The cloak of anonymity covering the painter's identity and position is retrieved by the standards and effects of that 'objective' distance dominating much of what has passed and continues to pass for therapy in mental health care. It is thanks to Freud's momentous discovery of the transferential dynamic Dora was living through at the time of her treatment and the ways in which it implicated him as both individual and function, and the ways in which it pinned him to that function, that the third has been introduced at the heart of the analytic relationship. Since its introduction, the articulation of this third has varied depending on orientation and focus; some have fixed it in terms of the space that unfolds in the encounter between analyst and analysand, the transitional space of play and association as Ogden would put it; others, most notably the Lacanians, have ascribed to it the status of a structural ground, as language and its laws for instance, without which the encounter would not even be possible; others still have identified it in terms of the institutional and professional codes internalized by the analyst under the heading of a clinical superego and/or ego ideal. Chronological and logical orders aside, it has become quite evident that no assessment of the events in a consulting room or a session is complete without its triadic dimensions, without, in other words, the axes of reference to which the one and the two are pinned.

In the context of the Fontainebleau painting, and were we to count to three, we would then have to recognize a certain void and fill it with a producer who is the subject of a desire for the two women, who may also be subject to their desire, and/or subject to the same desire that is theirs; Ursula Brändli's recent *Trockenkreide* is a case in point. Were we to count to three, we would then have to unleash the very desire to count and multiply, and, as Bonnet has pointed out, over 130 artists in the twentieth century alone have already beaten us to that count (*Les deux amies*, 322). Clinically, we have indeed continued with the counting to unravel the multi-layered qualities of the characters we typically identify as analyst and analysand. An appreciation of the counter-transference has taught us that it is not only the analysand's associations that are the objects of an analysis. Also, an understanding of the process as, at one level at least, an apprenticeship in a method and a style of self-understanding has implied that it is not only the analyst who is its subject. We have come to recognize that both parties participate in both roles dynamically, unevenly and not always altogether predictably. Relevant to this context are the ways in which we have followed in the footsteps of Harold Searls,[79] for instance, and gone on to complicate the scenario even further by suggesting that, among its various roles, the unconscious of the analysand functions not only as object of an analysis but as its supervisor as well. And on it goes, in the most faithful of approaches to the psychoanalytic understanding of a field as inherently multi-layered and over-determined.

Inevitable as it may be, my counting is running a little ahead of itself here and so I would like to go back to the couplet conversion hysteria/passing disability and suggest that the two-dimensional schema with which I started, the schema that understands them as quasi-specular reflections of one another, lacks a certain perspectival depth. Indeed, every reflection requires a holding place for the mirror-like surface that makes it possible. As much as hysteria may become a disability and disability may be the ground or subject for a hystericization, both categories point to a third that is the supposedly healthy and able observer/intervener. Instead of the mirror reflections or images of each other, hysteria and disability are better understood as the filtered and hence exaggerated representations of the so-called normal, which is to say anonymous, third; the third that has depicted them as mannequin-like, which is to say lifeless; the third that is often the motor force behind the presumed objectivity and transparency for much of what passes as clinical vignette and case study.

A little over 6 decades after the Fontainebleau painting, enters the Dutch master Johannes Vermeer. In his case for the artist's use of the camera obscura, Philip Steadman reconstructs studio, subjects and scenes in order to locate the positions and perspectives in Vermeer's work. Steadman's intent here is to neither disparage nor diminish the master's talent but to highlight his curiosity and inventiveness, as well as his willingness to experiment with his day's latest discoveries in geometry and optics. A case in point is *The Music Lesson* as it deploys some of the key elements of a photographic reproduction dependent on a discreet point of view, discreet in its specificity as well as in its quasi-absence from the frame. Steadman's perspective analysis uncovers the scene's central vanishing point as well as the theoretical viewpoint Vermeer had presumably occupied while composing his work (*Vermeer's Camera*, 75–77). The play of perspective here is not without its ironies: as much as he wished to extract himself from his subject matter by depicting it in a realist and photographic style, Vermeer is not oblivious to his role in the composition for he will go so far as to include himself in the work through the subtle reflection of his easel and canvas in the mirror above the virginals.

Lest my presentation be mistaken for an endorsement of a progressivist or developmental aspect to the history of artistic production, I would like to introduce a third moment here, one whose beginnings date from roughly a little over 6 decades prior to the Fontainebleau episode. In 1534, the newly installed Pope Paul III ordered Michelangelo to commence work on the Sistine Chapel altarpiece, *The Last Judgement.* Two of the piece's compositional and perspectival qualities are critical here. The first is the forward incline at which the artist had insisted the wall behind the alter be rebuilt in order to create in the worshipping audience a sense of the fresco's overwhelming grandeur and the power of its subject matter. With 2,000 square feet of an awe-inspiring work whose bottom is at about a foot away from the vertical, one is not simply standing in front of a masterpiece of human production but in the space of an engulfing superhuman presence and authority at the end of history itself. Moreover, and as Loren Partridge notes, the fresco's innovative lack of a frame 'promotes, as none had before, the illusion of a non-existent wall and the Second Coming's unfolding in real time before the worshippers' very eyes' ('Michelangelo's Last Judgement', 17). Coupled with such weight and enormity is yet another compositional trick that no artist had attempted before: in placing the gaping mouth of hell right behind the altar, Michelangelo leaves no doubt in the mind of the worshipper and spectator as to the artist's impression of the last judgement awaiting the temporal representative of said enormity. Michelangelo's ironic imprint on each and every mass henceforth celebrated in the chapel testifies to the bitter friction that governed his relationship to the papacy, a friction that has not ceased to exert much academic curiosity and concentration.

These works of Vermeer and Michelangelo introduce the third as the observer who is invariably implicated in the observation. At times the producer who cannot but betray his position and perspective and at others the consumer for whose benefit the work has been designed and executed, this third is neither singular nor uncomplicated. Similarly, and in the clinical context, we have come to appreciate that the free associations are never two-dimensional, factual or historical accounts but enactments of key principles and phantasies that engage both producer and consumer, analysand and analyst.

At this point, I would like to extend the line of this perspectival history from the Renaissance to the works of a Picasso who, in *Les demoiselles d'Avignon*, for instance, multiplies the privileged viewpoints to such an extent that one is no longer in a position to deny the fact of the privilege and its complexity. Picasso's is not simply the painting of a number of women each constructed from her own perspective but of a number of women each constructed from a number of perspectives, differently, simultaneously. We clinicians at this point are also quite aware of the concurrence of a number of transference/counter-transference vectors and perspectives that are at work at any given point in the treatment. Rather than a single dynamic that is at times duplicated and at others reversed in the style of Heinrich Racker's concordance and concomitance,[80] we understand, as for instance Christopher Bollas does,[81] the interplay of a multitude of such transferential vectors and their simultaneous psychodynamic impacts.

I have one last non-analytic point to make before I return to the hysteria/disability material. The point is actually Arthur I. Miller's in his recent study of Picasso and Einstein.[82] Miller makes a convincing parallel between artist and physicist, and by extension between cubism and relativity theory, not for the sake of an interplay or commerce between art and science but in order to expose a broader cultural and intellectual surround in which both have been implicated. The surround in question revolves around the modes and limits of human knowledge, around what exists and what is seen, how it is seen or not seen and how it is communicated as having been seen or not seen, a surround that has also been the conduit for the development of psychoanalysis as the science of the unconscious as unseen but not any the less knowable.

In this respect, psychoanalysis has exposed the severe myopia regarding the unconscious from which the conventions of both psychology and psychiatry have suffered. Sadly but not too surprisingly, psychoanalysis is now suffering these two disciplines' retaliatory resentment and humiliation. In any case, and since the 1920s, painting went on to effect a move from a multi-perspectival Picasso to a figurative Kandinsky for whom non-representational, and hence non-perspectival, composition is much less an obstacle than a challenge, a necessity even. Likewise, physics has effected its own move from Einstein's relativity theory to Heisenberg's quantum mechanics and in the process from a science of representable objects to a science of relations between objects that are themselves inherently unavailable for representation.

Ironically, and notwithstanding its investment in quite a sophisticated relational model of exploration and treatment, contemporary psychoanalysis is still bound to its representational roots. The argument for such roots has gone something like this: the unconscious may not be seen but it is staged, made present and represented as the scene of transferential and counter-transferential dynamics at any particular analytic moment. In this context, the free associations are understood as at times a copy that re-presents and hence makes manifest the structures and dynamics of the original unconscious and at others the emissary or delegate of that unconscious, the one through which analytic intervention and negotiation are made possible. What would it then mean for psychoanalysis, not so much to abandon its representational strategies (for I am not calling for an abandonment of Einstein or Picasso or any of the scientists and artists that preceded them) but to supplant these strategies with the tools and insights that have since made a tremendous contribution to the intellectual and cultural surround? What would an analysis of the couplet transference/counter-transference consist of and produce under such circumstances? And, last but not least, how would any of the above impact our understanding and practice of the pinning of word to place and of mind to body? These are three very weighty questions whose answers I can only begin to untangle at this point.

Seeing

As much as a work of art participates in certain relations of power with, and is hence pinned to, its outside, it is equally the site for and an instantiation of its own peculiar configuration of forces – be they material, aesthetic, erotic, pedagogical, political or ethical. Such configurations serve as the modes by which the work's various components are made to relate to and influence one another, which is to say the modes in which such components are pinned to one another. It is the pinning of matter, perspective, idea, execution and delivery for instance that imbues the work with an artistic dimension, that, in other words, allows it to be something other than merely a political commentary, an ethical treatise, or an erotic depiction. The pinning is always operating at these two levels then: within and without.

Similarly, quantum mechanics has taught us that, though we are in no position to know an electron as such, as a thing in itself, we do have access to the relations of attraction and repulsion that govern its pinnings with other particles, that it is these pinnings and in turn our relations and pinnings to them that, strictly speaking, constitute the objects and contents of our knowledge. Note here that such knowledge is inscribed as a relation in its particular time and space as much as it is in a history or a genealogy. The relations that obtain between two individuals in an analytic context, the transferential and counter-transferential ways in which they are pinned to one another, are no doubt products of conflicts and deficits that precede both session and treatment. However, there is much more to the transference than a mere repetition or re-enactment of earlier and more original scenarios; there is also much more to the counter-transference, even if it is 'objective' as Winnicott would prefer it, than a mere compliment or echo of that transference. Both are inscribed in a broader network of relations, which is to say of pinnings, in the present of both treatment and session.

It is often argued that, no matter how subtle or complicated, the transference is a restaging and a repetition of the analysand's unresolved and/or unfulfilled wishes, that it is the repetition of a consciously unfamiliar but foundational history of wishes and relations. The transference is also considered the site of an incessant repetition, of an impasse the treatment is designed to clear. Though what occurs in this transference is in one respect the return of the same, what gives it its analytic quality and hence separates it from other instances of repetition is its grounding in the free associations as the occasion for unleashing an endlessly malleable series of connections and permutations, i.e. of pinnings, between words, affects, body parts and ideas. The analytic transference is identified much less by the return of a pathological situation and more by the fact that no matter how many connections and pinnings one traverses, there are many more that remain to be produced, experienced and spoken. Much like the recounting of a dream sequence whose analytic usefulness lies less in its quality as a refrain and more in its possibilities of addition, substitution and reordering, the analytic transference is defined less by a return of the same than it is by the return of the inexhaustibly multiplying different. The point holds for artistic production as opposed to the assembly line and for biological reproduction as opposed to cloning.

This is not the fetishization of the different and its valuation over and above the same, but the recognition of the fact that as much as the same is ever present, it is the different that constitutes singularity, analytic or otherwise. While never losing sight of the common denominator, psychoanalysis distinguishes itself from most other disciplines, theoretical and clinical, in its focus on that variation and in exploring the singular ways in which we as individuals live and can live our pinnings. In so doing, it elaborates and intervenes in the ways in which we confirm or break a pre-formed understanding of pinning, even if it be our own; in so doing, it realigns our understanding and practice of health much less as a specific type or form of pinning and more as a sustained readiness and agility to the fact of pinning.

The most analytic instance of this principle and manoeuvre that I have come across recently is a non-clinical text from 1998 by the writer Hélène Cixous, herself no stranger to the ambivalences and complexities of psychoanalysis. *Savoir* is a relatively short text in which Cixous articulates not only new ways for pinning word to place but, and more importantly, new ways in which a word can be made to pin different places to one another. Cixous deploys autobiography, religion, theory and poetic imagination to articulate a myopia that passes, which is to say a myopia that does not register with the fully sighted, and a myopia that is subject to surgical intervention and correction. She, Cixous, the myopic, could see that she could not see; her myopia was the 'little nail stuck in the gap' (6) between the worlds of vision and blindness, the nail that is simultaneously the cause for much pain as well as an occasion for the pinning and concurrence of two otherwise incommensurable worlds. As Cixous writes, myopic living is a state of alert where seeing is a 'tottering believing' and everything is 'perhaps' (6). Myopia is such that it cannot be seen by the seeing who, when confronted with it, are incredulous ('I would not have guessed!'), doubting ('But you manage so well!'), and hence unwilling to come to terms with their own inability to see that they cannot see. As 'the mistress of error' (7), myopia reigns supreme over one and all; as much as the invisible divider between the non-seeing and the seeing, it is the invisible connector that exposes our universal myopia.

Still, myopia for Cixous is a site and a sight not only of ambivalence, uncertainty and fear but also of that possibility from which the limits and ossifications of certainty and its myopia have been expelled. Indeed, if not-to-see is a deficit and a thirst, not-to-see-oneself-seen is a strength, an independence and a lightness (12), and hence a freedom from the constraint of the image of oneself that one sees in the eye of the other, that very same freedom that we analysts invite our analysands to explore, know, and cite through the use of the couch, that very same freedom that we often cherish for ourselves as they lie on that couch. Unwittingly, psychoanalysis participates in a practice that abstracts from myopia as a physiological limitation its virtue as an opening onto a site/sight and a citing that reconfigure the customary and conscious pinnings of self and other as well as of those of word and place and of mind and body. As a result, myopia is brought forth as neither an object nor a condition but as the mark of a complex set of relationships that one enters into while dealing with oneself and the world. Its psychological significance lies much less in its status as a pathology, a disability or a deficit and more in the ways in which it is deployed and the purposes it is made to serve, some of which, needless to say, may very well indeed be pathological. While at times a handicap, myopia is also a tool that opens onto the possibility of a pinning that is the analytic transference fraught with ambivalence and unpredictability, a transference governed by a sight/site, a citing and a knowledge that are forever in the making.

That, in at least one of its registers, psychoanalysis is an inherently myopic practice should come as a surprise to no one. The dynamic is in fact at the heart of one of its most inspiring of precedents. Indeed, and while a punishment to his incestuous and parricidal crimes, Oedipus's self-inflicted blindness, with pins no less, was also the opening onto that most sacred and untimely of sights/sites through which he could access a truth that would radically and forever redefine for him what it means to be worldly and knowledgeable. Presumably, and whether real or phantasized, his crime, guilt, punishment and redemption are often set up as the successive stages of our own analytic passages. What remains to be seen is the extent to which the pursuit of a psychoanalytic treatment nowadays needs to be confined to a retracing of its hero's pilgrimage from the gates of Thebes to his burial ground in the woods of Colonus; the extent to which such a pursuit is propelled by, or producing of, the unconscious phantasy of an Oedipal culpability as well as of a demand for an absolution or at the very least an alleviation of its accompanying guilt; and the extent to which the use of the couch is a re-enactment of the Sophoclean script, its recapitulation and re-inscription into a world that has presumably given up on the very idea of myth, eternity and absolution; the extent to which, in other words, the couch is deployed as an instrument of the analysand's exoneration by a blind or blinding but merciful analyst.

As much as none of this can be adequately articulated and worked through except in the context of a specific individual at a specific moment in his or her analysis, the following questions need to be raised: how much of this dynamic is still the outcome of a counter-transferential implantation and a pinning that, in the manner of a retrograde analysis, extrapolate from a punishment and a redemption, from a couch and an insight, the presence of a preceding crime and guilt? How much is the nature of the crime incestuous and parricidal? And how much of the guilt is indeed an offering and an appeasement? Put differently, how much is the individual analytic experience pinned onto the content and structure of a representation that has already been declared paradigmatic? And how much is such a representation, qua representation and regardless of its content, limiting of the pinning and its possibilities?

I have already addressed most of these questions in the preceding chapters. I would like now to focus on Cixous's contribution, more specifically on its title *Savoir*. The term references both the French word for knowledge as well as the verb *voir*, to see, preceded by the feminine declension of the possessive article, *sa*. Cixous's linguistic pinning of, supposedly, the masculine categories of knowledge, depth and power to the feminine as a preoccupation with surface, appearance and gaze uncovers their stereotypical and hence questionable determinations. This pinning also uncovers and makes seen our very need to see in order to distinguish between not only the abilities but the genders and their sexualities as well, for nothing makes us more uncomfortable than the inability to see the markers of such identifications, and nothing makes us more volatile, if not violent, than the inability to know to which of the categories their bearers belong. Invariably, the confusion remains ours as much as it may sometimes be theirs, and so does the responsibility to tolerate it. *Les deux amies* at Fontainebleau may be flat because their representation lacks a perspective; but perhaps it is precisely this lack that allows them a freedom and an opening to be themselves as not-seen, as not-seeing-themselves-seen and hence as forever yet-to-be-seen.

While transmogrified into an English Id as a proper noun, a privileged and hence, by the very exercise of its naming and pinning, a properly contained agency, Freud's *es* holds on to its most ubiquitous and common of characters with the French rendering *ça*. Another variation on Cixous's title is then the one that writes a *savoir* but also speaks and hears a *ça-voir*, an it-to-see, and hence a 'seeing' that belongs to and indeed defines as a gerund that which lies at the heart of the unconscious, and hence psychoanalytic, enterprise, a gerund that is only subsequently bifurcated into that which supposedly belongs to either a sa or a son, a feminine or a masculine, a ça or a son, an object or a sound.

'*Avant elle n'était pas une femme d'abord elle était une myope c'est-à-dire une masquée*' (17): 'Before she was not a woman first she was a myopic meaning one masked' (10). Cixous's refusal to punctuate her words 'properly', to fix them in a syntactical order and a structural hierarchy, which is also to say to pin them to a pre-formed gender, underscores the varied ways in which they are to be understood bodily, sensually, as they are read and/or heard. Depending on its pauses and stresses, 'Before she was not a woman first she was a myopic meaning one masked' could point to any one of the following:

- She was already myopic before she had become woman.
- While myopic and woman, the site of her primary difference lay in her sight and not in her genitalia.
- Myopia had afforded her a mask behind which she could be whatever woman she chose, if and when she chose.
- She is now the woman who had once been masked by her myopia.
- She had once held a myopic meaning that one masked.

These are but the beginnings of a potentially inexhaustible series of meanings that point to the instability not so much of meaning per se but of the gendered punctuations to which we have pinned it, forcibly, exclusively.

Indeed, much of what has been said and written of sexual difference over the past century ascribes it the status of an access code to most of what constitutes and is legitimized by, among others, feminism, psychoanalysis and cultural theory. Much remains to be written of that code's complications and ambivalences. In the meantime, what needs to be articulated is a reassessment of the very practice of coding as it pins to any difference, be it of gender, sexuality, ability, class, race, or what not, a primacy over and above any other bodily marker. In her *Savoir*, and whether intentionally or not, one has no easy way of telling, Cixous points to a network of markers that may be prioritized, i.e. given shape and perspective, only in relation to and in the context of a specific body and a specific life. Gone is the practice of investing this or that quality with a universal privilege, the one with which every therapeutic, intellectual and/or political project must comply, the one to which every move must be pinned. Cixous indeed opens the door onto a practice that is not only concerned with the specifics of a certain relationship between femininity and myopia, gender and vision, body and perspective, but with the implicit but not any the less crucial redefinition of the practice of pinning as inevitably and synchronically multiple.

Clinically, we have understood and practised the pinning of word to place and of psyche to soma as exclusively gendered. We have adamantly organized our notions of law and desire, of history and identity, around those physiological traits that mark us as male or female. We have glorified these traits, sanitized, disavowed, decried and sanctified them; we have traced their implications, tabulated their dangers, celebrated their privileges and suffered their failures. In this respect, there is hardly anything new to the claim that the pinning is multiple, that its modalities and purposes have varied according to the uses and values, agendas and intentions of the gendered individual to whom they belong. However, the multiplicity that Cixous's text points to, the one I would like to carry further, has as much to do with the locations and purposes of the pinning as it does with its intensities and qualities.

This brings me back to the perspectives and bodies that the history of artistic production has bequeathed us, be they presumably altogether nonexistent (as with the unsigned Fontainebleau or Kandinsky), singularly unified (as with Vermeer and Michelangelo), or synchronically multiple (as with Picasso). I would like to extend the moves and fluctuations of such a history to the psychoanalytic discourse on identity and its transferential echoes. I would like to suggest that, all too often, such a discourse has been enmeshed with the heading and perspective of gender difference at the expense of all others. The world of a Rome to which all the roads of geopolitics led, of a heavenly deity at which all redemptive supplications were directed, of an absolute knowledge to which all scientific inquiries aspired, and of a primary dynamic around which all bodily desires were organized, that is a world that is no longer ours, assuming, indeed, that it ever was. Rome, God, Truth and Oedipus have long since been unseated from their respective thrones. In their stead, we recognize not so much the radical absence of any singular organizational principle, for the claim to such an absence itself is singular and principled, but the simultaneous and incessant pull of a number of hubs and coordinates around which our practices have come to be organized.

In its hey day, Rome may have wished itself the sole centre of power and commerce; the fact of the wish itself speaks of an altogether different reality. Moreover, the empire has long since been displaced by a number of others, including itself under an unfamiliar and not entirely favourable guise; as much can be said of God, Truth and Oedipus. Of this we can be certain: no contender to a throne is without a match, and no throne is everlasting. Sexual difference has often claimed for itself the primary, indomitable and matchless ground and perspective upon which and through which are erected psyche, soma and, by extension, the channels via which these two have communicated. It has arrogated for itself the title of queen and has condemned any questioning of its primacy and supremacy as enmity, folly, blaspheme or misguided-ness. This has been the case for psychoanalysis as much as for feminism.

In the face of such despotism, one could advocate the overthrow of the powers that be in favour of a presumably more inclusive or even egalitarian structure that would accommodate the various bodily markers as legitimate sites of psychological identifications, differentiations and alliances. One could then argue that disability, and lack thereof, is potentially as constitutive of the unconscious and its dynamics as is gender. In its early years, a visually impaired or hard of hearing child, for instance, is as liable to endure the presence and absence of sight or sound as much as, if not more than, that of the penis. In a familial triangle marked by such a dynamic, the traffic in identification and ambivalence is shaped as much by the fact that some can see or hear while others can't as it is by the fact that some have a penis while others don't. The triangle is hence as much a triangle of ability as it is one of sex or gender. With some modification, the argument could also be extended to show how the same triangle is, at times, equally a triangle of race for instance. Any body part that is available for the child as a site of identification of self with other and differentiation between self and other is hence potentially yet another site of pinning and triangulation.

It is in this much more fundamental sense that the pinning of psyche to soma is synchronically multiple; its locations are not limited to the erogenous zones; they can and, as is becoming increasingly evident, they very often do include most organs, limbs, senses and skins. One could; but one shouldn't have to unless the material itself is such that the sites of psychological differentiation and pinning are indeed multiple. The despotism of multiplicity is no less stifling than that of uniformity.

Chapter Seven

Désirand: the transitional subject

A philosopher and a psychoanalyst once agreed that to love someone is to give them what one does not have and what they do not want. For both Plato and Lacan, what grounds such a love is an experience and a situation that produce in the beloved/analysand an insight into truth, truth that cannot be given but can be discovered, truth that is not needed but is desired. Crucial for this situation is the lover's own passion, the one that fuels Plato's *Elenchus* and Lacan's *desire of the analyst,* for it is this passion and not truth itself that is the object of the communication.

While tolerated for the meditatively inclined, such talk of love and passion may seem a luxury, a distraction or even a seduction replete with its own set of dangerous, and perhaps even illicit, pleasures. After all, such talk is occurring in the context of a treatment that is often predicated on its capacity to alleviate suffering, to restore, or in-store, a modicum of health and balance or, at the very least, a respite from misery. The difficult if not at times unbearable irony is that precisely because talk of love may seem superfluous and/or offensive that it can be of the highest psychoanalytic import. This is one reason why I am opting to speak here of love and not of its more tolerable and tameable cousin 'care'. The other reason lies in the current commodification of such 'care', in its registration as deliverable and exchangeable, in its identification as a prescriptive marker that separates those that have it from those that need it, or those that give it from those that don't deserve it.

To speak of love is to speak not of merit and resources but of desire and its truth. Such a desire is never solipsistic and it does not pertain to some lofty, amorphous and generalized category such as 'humanity' or 'thought' or 'health' or 'poetry'. To speak the truth of this desire is to do so in the context of a distinct situation or encounter between specific individuals, in their individualities rather than in their identifications or affiliations. Such identifications may indeed help us designate community memberships and relational similarities and differences; they may also organize and consolidate exchange and/or conflict within a group or across groups at any given point in time. But they can tell us virtually nothing of the individual as individual, of the singular ways in which it negotiates its relations of identity and difference, of attraction and repulsion, of the ways in which it makes them explicit for its own self as well as for others and of the ways in which it uses them; in other words, of the ways in which this individual desires.

Put differently, and while we as humans may share the overwhelming substance of our genetic and psychological make-up, it is that infinitesimally minuscule residue that makes us individuals, not in opposition or similarity to others, but in who we are and what we are, not as peculiarities, deviations or alternatives but as singular and positive qualities. Put differently, again, but this time psychoanalytically, talk of dynamics (pre-, post-, or anti-oedipal), transferences (positive, negative, concordant or symbolic), and positions (schizoid, psychotic or perverse) may allow us a generalized though nonetheless highly useful, if not indispensable, map of the psyche's terrain. But, and like any such map, it cannot give us a point by point account of that terrain; it in fact cannot but reach the limit that separates the formalized from the individual and the specific. Our task then is to recognize that map's limit, reconcile with the inevitable fact of its, and its limit's, presence, and, if we are so inclined, cross it by traversing the terrain itself.

This is how I understand psychoanalysis, as an instance of such a traversal by means of a process of free associations and through an experience of the transference. I would like to speak of this traversal, of its detours, textures and energies, of the transformations it effects in both traveller and terrain, and of its implications for the art of map-making. My communication is not of immutable or universal truths, for, no doubt, my text too will have to contend with its own limits. What I would like to do instead is to propose a series of postulates that will help draw a provisional outline of the situation, of its experience and of its rootedness in the desires of those that produce and participate in it, the desires we generally recognize as lying at the core of their ways of being and of their identities.

While I draw extensively on the material of the previous chapters, I do not consider my observations here as their definitive conclusions. Instead, these are among the metapsychological instances of what Deleuze and Guattari term the conjunctive ('so that's what it is!') synthesis. I locate them at one point of intersection between the psychoanalytic and the schizoanalytic, at the point at which I have chosen to pin these two orientations to one another. As such, they may carry much that is already familiar; however, and hopefully, they may also carry an element of productivity, at least in terms of their clinical and/or theoretical momentum. Obviously, they will also carry the potential to frustrate and perhaps even infuriate. I do not absolve myself of the responsibility for their frustrations nor do I claim for myself alone the credit for their possible rewards; in both, the reader is often my partner.

Chronology

Identity and desire are pointers to sexuality,[83] at least for many of us at this point in our history. The cluster of questions concerning love, transference, desire, identity and most of whatever else we may wish to consider under the heading of 'analysis', is inevitably implicated in a set of experiences and understandings of time and of sexuality as inscribed in it. I say 'set of experiences' here to introduce the notion that, indeed and sometimes much to our chagrin, the experience we have of time, and by extension of sexuality, is invariably multiple.

To begin, chronological time; the time of past, present and future; the time with which we are most familiar but also the time with which we have struggled the most since its past has been immune to our interventions and its future beyond our predictions. We have countered such a time with a barrage of strategies such as

- philosophic, as in a platonic form that lies outside the time of imitation;
- religious, as in an unmoved deity outside the time of transience;
- and technological, as in a practical knowledge outside the time of uncertainty.

Periodically, we have wished to remove ourselves as observers from the continuum and directionality of chronology at least long enough to trace sexuality's history, either at the level of the species (across periods and cultures in their transitions, degenerations, and/or breaks) or at the level of the individual (across libido's so-called developmental stages). Alternatively, we have wished to remove sexuality as object of observation from chronology's continuum by grounding it in a quasi-immutable essence, genetic code or psychological structure. In all these cases, our wish has been that, finally, on some future day, all will be clarified and all will be given. Our experience of chronological time has thus always carried with it a yearning for the timeless.

As of late, we have resorted to thinking sexuality as functioning in a time where nothing is given, not in the sense of an absence of definitions, laws or restrictions but in the sense of a sexuality that appears as a given when in fact it is but the enactment of a script that produces it and which it in turn perpetuates, a script that may very well be available for change. Sexuality is now declared the product of disparate discourses and disciplines whose powers and interests it is made to serve. Sexuality is in conversation with its time; it is recognized as not only institutionalized and repetitive, but also institutionalizing and disciplinarian; sexuality is, in other words, performative.[84]

While telling of certain conceptual needs and underpinnings, all of these theories of sexuality give their readers and/or producers very little by way of a hint as to how they are to make sense of their own sexualities in the everyday of their experiential unfolding. Unlike theoretical physics or the study of macro-economic trends, the demand has often been that the discourse on sexuality be accessible and personally relevant.[85] However, a map cannot but render its terrain as incomplete and provisional. Any talk of sexuality that lays a claim to thoroughness, that, in other words, presumes to satisfy the requirements of particularity and accuracy is by that very same token suspect. To be given its due, the demand for personal relevance has to be thwarted first. The project for a discourse on sexuality, very much like that for a theory, a literature, a science and an art, is inevitably and frustratingly anti-democratic, at least insofar as its legitimacy and merit ought to lie outside the confines of an inherent ability to speak to, or on behalf of, the multitude. By that same token, such a project is the closest to the spirit of democracy in its insistence on individual specificity, relevance and meaning and in its corresponding resistance to the rule of the majority. It is for this reason that a discourse on sexuality is accurate only insofar as it recognizes its lack of accuracy in the face of the particular. Put positively, a discourse on sexuality is accurate only insofar as it provides us with whatever tools we require to explore and articulate subsequently and for ourselves the particular as positive, full and particular. Alfred Jarry's pataphysics as a science of the particular, as opposed to the generalities of its meta-physical counterpart, and hence as an examination concerning the laws of exceptions,[86] is a wonderfully humorous, but no less apt, parallel here. Transference is what I know. Transference is what I do. I shall speak of it as the occasion for a pata-analysis.

The Unconscious

'I dreamt I was trying to cremate my mother but she kept nagging at me that I wasn't doing a proper job;' 'I dreamt I was standing by the curb watching children board a bus; I knew they were all going to die; I was horrified and I just sat there doing nothing and feeling nothing.' Mother is both dead and alive; horror and apathy inhabit the same moment. These two dream fragments illustrate the ways in which the unconscious typically breaks through the laws of chronology via the simultaneity and superposition of the representations of events and affects. A dream tells us not only of the inner workings of the unconscious – displacement, condensation and secondary revision being three of its frequently invoked dynamics – but also of one of its most conservative and yet most fruitful qualities: the unconscious admits of no negation or refuse; in it nothing ever dies; it manipulates our past not as a once-upon-a-time that, on occasion, may bear an impact on our present, but as a present that is ever deployed and ever invested.

A dream is not a succession but an overlay of images. The supposed order of its frames is but a revision registered by its telling; it is the making explicit and accessible of one form of an apparently non-sensical unconscious thought to, and through, another that is manifest, sequential and graspable; it is a traversal of sorts, from one thought to another, from one mode of being to another. Like any such traversal, this revision admits of both losses and gains. It is in the transference that the analysand's unconscious mode of thinking and being, of traversing is made most explicit. Indeed, the transference is the lived effect of the inner workings of the free associations as these mobilize and trigger the dynamics that underlie certain types of knowledge. While the analyst is effectively that mode's most explicit and readily available object, what the transference ultimately enacts is much more of the analysand's way of thinking and being toward him or herself in those parts that have yet to be spoken and explored.

When productive, the experience of such a transference brings to its fullest the measure of a particular and individualized constellation of psychic work; it resonates with it and reveals it in its untimely-ness. It achieves this through the tense and disconcerting confrontation with the unconscious, as outside chronological time and hence as un-timely, in the context of a practice that is thoroughly suffused with chronology: in a most elemental sense (sequencing of words and meanings); in a technical sense (timing of interventions and terminations; conceptual elaborations of defences as fixations or regressions along timed, developmental lines); in a practical sense (length and frequency of sessions; payment schedules; extra-analytic contact).

Jean-Bertrand Pontalis has suggested that the time of psychoanalysis is not a negation of chronology as is the case with the timeless and its disciplinary advocates philosophy, religion and science. Much like the dream's relationship to sleep, Pontalis writes that the time of psychoanalysis is rather the accomplishment of chronology (*Ce temps qui ne passe pas*, 26). Of course, the risk that the practice has run often is to turn its frames and dynamics into the accomplices of, at times, the strictest of chronologies, not only clinically but politically as well.[87] Such a risk notwithstanding, the point that is most relevant for me here is that the transference enacts the untimely quality of the unconscious and of sexuality, their disorganization of the time we manifestly know and live, not in favour of a timeless and static absolute but as a site of sheer irreverence for the laws of succession and fixity.[88] In an initial move, the transference disrupts our experience of time as either chronological or absolute and of sexuality as either developmental or preset. In the process, this transference makes possible a betrayal of the generalized logic of opposites and exclusivity, the same logic that has permeated our practices of identity – bodily, politically and intellectually (health/pathology, masculinity/femininity, self/other, heterosexuality/homosexuality).

In a second and more fundamental move, and rather than an accomplishment, the transference opens onto a time that the Romans once recognized in Janus. The gates to his temple are open at times of war, where beginning and end collide, when the split between past and future, reality and phantasy, self and other is no longer necessary. With Janus, simultaneity becomes a crisis only from the point of view of the logic of borders and exclusions. At such a moment and in such a time, the task of being either here or there or of being on the way from here to there gives way to the experience of being both here and there, of inhabiting different spaces, thoughts and identities simultaneously. The traversal between conscious and unconscious is always folded back onto itself. As in the time of war, there is much room for fear and confusion; unlike the time of war, there is also much room for movement and possibility. The linearity of the hierarchy between who one is and what one chooses to be (conveniently, strategically or defensively), the linearity, if not comfort, of passing is unsettled when Janus has both his faces turned in the same direction, when, in seeing the double, he sees the depth. It is in this topological rather than archeological sense that depth enters the psychoanalytic experience.

Transference

The work of free association in the analytic session consists of two simultaneous moves: dis-association and re-association; it is the loosening and reconfiguring of the ties and sequences produced by the linguistic rendering of the primary process. In the words of Jean Laplanche, this is the work of 'de-translation' and 're-translation' in which the analyst functions less as the upholder of rigour and accuracy and more as the provider of whatever tools are necessary for the analysand to pursue the traversal and for the work to proceed.[89]

As much as they may evoke a history and a wish, the transference and the free associations also offer an occasion for the elaboration of different scenarios and intensities. They may tell not only of what was and of what should have or might have been instead, but also of all that has yet to be, and, most poignantly, of the fact that much may never even begin to be. They uncover the psyche's deep-seated organizing principles, its rigidly instituted knowledge. In the process, they expose a certain ignorance and a false sense of completeness that are constitutive of a primary process that has been reified, deadened even, by the exclusionary disjunctions of its secondary counterpart.

It is often argued that, no matter how subtle or complicated, the transference is a restaging and a repetition of the analysand's unresolved and/or unfulfilled wishes, that it is the repetition of a consciously unfamiliar but nonetheless endemic organization of wishes and relations. In such a schema, the transference is considered the site of a clogging or a jam in the form of a repetition of the same that the treatment is designed to clear. The metaphors of the analyst as plumber or traffic officer do carry a certain relevance and utility; however, and on the one hand, they miss out on much of what is available in terms of conduits for the processing of traffic and waste; and, on the other hand, they institute the sustained internalization of the cop or the plumber as necessary conditions for the success of the treatment.

Though what occurs in the transference is in one respect the return of the same under the guise of earlier scenarios and dynamics, what separates it from other instances of repetition, what, in other words, identifies it as a specifically analytic construct and hence invests it with clinical potential is its expression of the presence and return of the different, a different that is occasioned by the person of the analyst and constituted by the associations themselves. In the time of chronology, exclusive disjunction is the order of the day; one is often pressured to make decisions as to which of any two alternatives is the case: either inside or outside and either before or after. One thus finds oneself recounting the frames of a dream as a linear series of images and events. When confusion and uncertainty strike, they are frequently experienced as the disconcerting signs of a failure in either memory or reasoning. But this failure, this breaking down or slip, is the effect of the untimely-ness of the unconscious, of its capacity to produce an endlessly malleable series of connections and disjunctions, and of its infinite permutations on the arrangements of the frames that are themselves too many to count, for they have been accruing over a lifetime of impressions and events. The failure is an opening onto new arrangements of words and of ideas, of new ways of being and of further associations.

The analytic transference is characterized much less by the return of a pathological projection or projective identification – as opposed to the hoped for emergence of a healthy mode of presence and expression – and more by the incessant fact that no matter how many modes and manoeuvres one traverses, there is still much that remains to be explored, experienced and spoken, there is still much that is not known and that may never be known. To my mind, it is this understanding and experience of the transference that distinguishes psychoanalysis from all the other psychotherapeutic modalities. While, at their best, the latter take on the task of helping their patients tell a history of conflicts and deficits and in so doing give meaning to the present and liberate it from its subservience to the past, psychoanalysis for its part challenges the very notion of the cognition of a singular and supposedly accurate chain of events as the culmination of the treatment. Its pivot is the breakdown or ossification of such history making.[90]

Indeed, and instead of lacking or biased in knowledge and justifications, the analysand frequently enters the treatment overly attached to a neurotic knowledge of causes and effects that no longer makes any sense, or instead to a borderline knowledge of splits and dissociations that makes too much sense. In either case, this knowledge is fixed in its consistency and completeness to the point where it is thoroughly devastated by its surprising exceptions. Rather than the return of the same, the analytic transference coincides with the return of the fact that there is so much more that is not being explored. Its resolution, if one can still use the term at all, is hence not in the substitution of the pathological with the healthy, or of the mistaken with the accurate, for that would be tantamount to the foreclosure or displacement of the problem and complication; instead of being stuck with and ossified around one configuration (the 'pathological'), one is henceforth stuck with and ossified around another (the 'healthy'). While such a manoeuvre often does count for an improvement we should be loathe to belittle, it is liable to achieve its objective only in a short or limited term for the 'healthy' too will sooner or later come up against its own problems and limitations.

Much of the clinical literature on the topic of transference has tended to focus on an enumeration of as exhaustive a list as possible of the principal transferential characters and positions that the analysand introduces into the session: child, sibling, law maker, educator, twin, confessor, provider. A list of corresponding counter-transferential functions is often lagging merely a few keystrokes behind. My concern is not so much that the lists so far compiled have not been useful or exhaustive enough, but rather that they have attempted exhaustibility when the attempt itself cannot but be doomed to failure from exhaustion. An analysis is nowhere near analytic unless it has begun to unravel and elucidate for both parties the particular, unique and hence unpredictable ways in which the analysand pursues and lives his or her primary processes, neither in similarity to other analysands nor in difference from them; neither in accordance with a previously articulated list of possible scripts, nor in defiance of such a list.

Every analysis offers both of its participants the opportunity to live and learn an idiosyncratic set of relations rather than to verify or reinforce an already existing one. To speak of such relations is to speak of the localized and partial subjectivities, transferential and counter-transferential, the participants take on and of the uses each will make of them. In this context, the clinical guideline lies in the furthering and multiplication of the re-associations and, by extension, of the uses the analysand makes of the analyst. Does what I say or do help open for my analysand new connections, images or associations? Does it foster or hinder the transference? Does it recast the analysand as a new and unexpected persona and/or function or does it cement lifelong or all-too-familiar schema? Do I, correspondingly, experience myself being used or deployed in ways that are specific to this individual and this analysis? The aim here is not the broadening of an affective or relational repertoire so that it may reach a previously established 'healthy' range; nor is the aim newness for its own sake; the aim is the discovery of the specific and the particular, of what is individual to the analysand and, by extension, to the relationship between the two participants. Malady is invariably specific. The same must be held of the process of analysing it, of attaining a so-called state of health and of the forms and contents of that health. It is for such reasons that many analysts have come to rightly appreciate that no two analyses are, or even can be, the same.

As for the resolution of the transference, it coincides with the moment when the analyst becomes redundant, when the analysand has acquired a capacity for the continued traversal from one scenario to another and the substitution of one scenario with another; which is to say a capacity to participate consciously in at least two modes of thought, and in the process to not only tolerate and survive but also thrive in the surprises, losses and gains that such a participation will invariably produce. Hence, and rather than truth, it is agility and resilience that make up the basic components of what I understand by the psychoanalytic cure. Such a cure is hardly the flag or guarantee of a completion; at best, it is akin to a measure of an immunity or a tolerance for the pain of inevitable incompletion, including that of the process of immunization itself.

Identity

Sexually, one may identify in one's everyday as homo-, bi-, hetero-, trans- or ambi-sexual; as celibate, polygamous or perverse. One may choose the extent to which such identifications are played out culturally, politically or economically. Indeed, the marks of orientation and modality, of object and aim, have become crucial in the secondary order of identity and group membership. However, on the couch, such orders are eclipsed by the subjectivities that the free associations open onto and that the transferences produce, subjectivities that are much subtler and more malleable and transient than those one encounters at the legislature, the parade or the office. This is not to suggest that the latter are meaningless or ineffectual but that they are hardly ubiquitous.

As the transference's permutations on characters and functions multiply, so do the relations of attraction and repulsion through which they are negotiated. Both parties emerge in their capacities as lovers in the Platonic/Lacanian sense with which this chapter opened, and as they do so, they also emerge as enemies.[91] The flow of associations mobilizes the primary phantasies of the relations that unsettle the secondary identifications of gender and orientation; in them one is no longer simply either masculine or feminine, either heterosexual or homosexual; more often than not, one is simultaneously all of the above and much more. As much as the untimelyness of the unconscious disorganizes the sequence of relations, it multiplies their corresponding subject-positions.

It is for this reason that the project for a 'cure' of homosexuality for instance, a project that has preoccupied much of the North American branch of analytic practice is misguided. Rather than merely testifying to a noxious and reactionary blindness to the ethical and cultural priorities of its liberal surround, the work of a Socarides, a Friedman or a Trop and Stolarow[92] betrays the core psychoanalytic elaboration of the unconscious as an untimely process and of primary libidinal object-choice as mobile and polyvalent, an elaboration we have yet to fully explore and comprehend, let alone surpass.

Associations

The method of free association was Freud's own response to one of the most challenging tasks with which psychoanalysis has had to grapple over its history: the elaboration of a system of contact, traversal and translation between the primary and secondary processes as two ways of thinking, and hence as two ways of being, that are radically alien to one another. In their elaborations of the unconscious, Lacanism and Ego Psychology seem to stand on the opposite ends of a conceptual scale that pits the ineluctable foreignness of the absolute symbolic against the domesticity of a chronological development. One recognizes the effects of such theorizing in the tone of the texts as well: from the turgidly undecipherable to the rigidly banal. What a shame it is to have reduced the workings of the unconscious to the structures of language or the chronologies of development, and to have colonized the former with the disciplines and strategies of either of the latter. Of such sad manoeuvres, Lacan was no less guilty than his ego-psychological brethren. Though the man read and spoke many languages, his theory was consummately monolingual and its violence lies much less in its translations and revisions than in its arrogant refusal to recognize and sustain their transformations and distortions and to give then their due.

Adopting the Freudian dictum that the psyche knows no distinction between reality and fantasy, Klein for her part chose to altogether bracket so-called 'external reality' and focus instead on the mechanics and progressions of unconscious phantasy. While relying heavily on Klein, Winnicott was the first to articulate the fact of an in-between that facilitates and organizes the passages between subjective and objective, self and other. Neither a hallucination nor a concretization, the Winnicottian 'transitional' object is the site of infantile illusion and, by extension, adult creativity. It is neither simply given nor autocratically created; it is a found object in the sense that, while belonging to an external reality, it is invested with the qualities that suit the momentary psychodynamic purposes of the individual that 'finds' it. It becomes 'transitional' at the very moment of its finding. Such an object bears the functional echoes of the fetish that Freud had identified as a product of repudiation that presumably saves its producer from psychosis as the worst of all possible fates.[93]

Of all the principal figures in the psychoanalytic pantheon, and in spite of the ideological restrictions of his parental metaphors, Winnicott is perhaps one of the most insightful of Freudians; the 'transitional' object as a site of illusion and creativity testifies to its author's investment in free associating as not simply an investigative clinical tool but as a necessary strategy for a 'healthy' mode of living. Rather than upon the uncovering of history, the enunciation of truth, the resolution of conflict or the mastery over anxiety, it is upon the capacity for play, or *bricolage* as Deleuze and Guattari would put it, that Winnicott bases his principal mark of health; instead of merely a tool for analytic inquiry, the capacity to associate freely has now been clearly identified as the goal of that inquiry. To take it one step further, the analytic moment occurs when the analyst makes his or her self available to the analysand as a 'transitional' subject to be 'found' and deployed creatively and when the analysand in turn 'finds' such a subject and, in the process, discovers his or her own subjectivity as equally transitional.

Counter-transference

Let me backtrack a little bit before I go any further. What can the analytic experience, instead of simply the theory of such an experience, tell us of transitional subjectivities and of the sexualities they pursue? Echoing Pontalis, the couch does not provide for the conciliation between the time of chronology and the untimely-ness of the unconscious; nor is that couch an instrument of resolution or a site of conquest. On the couch, through the transference, and by means of free associations, what is made explicit and negotiated is the tension of a situation on which have converged at least three modalities of time and, by extension, of sexuality: the chronological/developmental, the timeless/identitarian and the untimely/disorganized.

While fleeting and momentary, the analytic moment is fundamentally tied to a specific topography, to a location that is initially provided by the analyst but subsequently taken over and re-mapped by both analyst and analysand. It is not so easily available for duplication in the shower or on a walk. It is predicated on the analysand's encounter not so much with the other as it manifests itself either in the person and function of the analyst as substitute parent or through the so-called Other that is the unconscious and its symbolic structures. The analytic situation is predicated on the analysand's encounter with the free associations he or she produces in the company of an other. Free association is a tool that brings to light the contact and exchange between, on the one hand, an individual's primary and secondary processes and, on the other hand, the primary process of one individual with that of an other's. What is most original, most difficult to deploy and most often overlooked about this tool is that it works most effectively when both analyst and analysand are engaged in it.

The caricature of the analyst at the edge of his or her seat vigilantly awaiting the slip, the dream or the turn of phrase that will once and for all unravel an analysand's Oedipal core has long outlived its use. The analyst is not an onlooker who judges the analysand's utterings according to some universal standards of health and accuracy. The analyst listens to the associations with 'an evenly suspended attention', as the saying goes, in order to open in him or herself a parallel series of associations. The suspension is indicative of neither benign impartiality nor disciplined reserve; what is suspended is the need to know in order to fix and predict, and the need to understand in order to diagnose and cure. The analyst's primary responsibility is to provide whatever tools are necessary for the analysand to pursue the associations and for the work to continue. Interpretations and insights are hence neither oracular truths nor verbal analgesics; they are conjunctive syntheses ('so that's what it is!') that allow both participants to effect shifts in thought, perception or experience, which is to say shifts in the ways they deploy themselves, separately and together, for themselves and for others. Interpretations and insights are transitional objects that multiply the connections between the associations and produce new syntheses and experiences. They make such multiplications and productions possible. In doing so, they produce new subjectivities that are themselves transitional.

While it initially starts out as the analysand's, the proprietary stamp on the free associations is transformed: the moment the words are uttered, the stamp becomes illegible. The words and the associations exist in that space of in-between that is neither simply the analyst's nor the analysand's. To a certain extent, either could lay partial claim to them – as producer or instigator – and yet neither could be fully confident in laying such a claim. 'These are my associations. I have spoken them. And yet, I would not had I not been here, with you. They are both mine and not mine. Does that make any sense?' The words occupy a space of participation where both parties are confronted with the ambiguously connective logic of me and not me, mine and not mine. The associations intersect, feed off and redirect one another. Both parties deploy the flows of words in order to generate further flows. This is why the trust and intimacy at the heart of the psychoanalytic alliance lie not in the telling of secrets but in the indeterminacy that is shared through the production of associations in the presence of another. This me and not me, mine and not mine logic resists the consolidation of a homogeneous and proprietary identity, be it of an individual, a couple or a group. It is important to stress the indeterminacy here since, ostensibly, the shared production is neither by nor of a unified and homogenous 'we'. This 'we' is bound to pit the couplet analyst-analysand against a 'they' that presumably lies outside the analytic situation. This 'we' is an instrument of identification (either similar or different), demarcation (either here or there), and affiliation (either inside or outside); it knows very little of indeterminacy.

One clinical implication here is that the often-debated questions of disclosure, its merits and its dangers, need to be recalibrated. As much as the analyst is more concerned with the unconscious dynamics of the analysand than with the particulars of the everyday (or, rather, with the latter primarily insofar as they reverberate with the former), the analysand is much more likely to appreciate and use an analyst who is being him or herself in the associations and interventions regardless of how much or how little he or she discloses. 'You may know very little about me; but I am being myself with you;' if spoken and when meant, such words are both reassuring of a certain integrity and releasing of the societal responsibility for curiosity.

Another equally significant clinical implication pertains to the fact that, as much as both analyst and analysand may lay claim to the associations, neither can do so independently of the other. The connective logic of me and not me, mine and not mine must hence demand from both participants a measure of relinquishment. On the side of the analysand, such a measure is indeed premised on the experience of a therapeutic alliance that confirms the analyst as present, understanding and trustworthy enough to be allowed by the analysand into his or her intricacies. On the side of the analyst, the relinquishment of words, associations and/or insights is possible only once the condition that the analysand is not so much assumed but experienced and accepted as an individual in his or her own right has been met. The dynamics of a therapeutic alliance must by definition involve the participation of more than one party and the conditions of trust as they have figured in the literature on the transference are hence no less significant in their counter-transferential details.

A third clinical implication emerges regarding such counter-transferential details. At this stage, I can offer only the rudiments of an elaboration. There is a layer to the preposition *gegen* in *Gegenübertragung* (counter-transference) that exceeds the logic of opposition or causality,[94] a layer that suggests instead contact and support (as in *lehnen gegen*/to lean against). No matter how 'sufficiently analysed', the analyst's experience and work cannot be reduced to that of a screen, a container or a recycling plant as an effect of or a response to the analysand's projections, splits or toxins. The two chains of associations, the analyst's and the analysand's, 'lean' against one another in the sense that they intersect, feed off and sustain one another. They are pinned to one another, which means that they can be pinned differently or that they are at times altogether unpinned. Fundamentally, the transference and counter-transference attract, repel, register and produce. As what cannot but remain unsaid, as the lived residue of all that has been said, they operate in the manner of two electrons, as in Feynman's diagram, unrepresentable but not any the less productive of a light quantum that is the insight as a conjunctive synthesis, as a 'so that's what it is!'

Grammar

Much of the impetus behind the psychoanalytic attempts at resolving the tensions and contradictions between conscious and unconscious, as two forms of thought and hence as two ways of being, has been fuelled by the dilemma of opposites manifest and latent, self and other, singular and plural. This dilemma is the effect of a surround that has plagued linguists, ethicists, and political theorists as much as it has psychoanalysts. Rights, obligations and priorities: these are but a few of the code words along which has navigated many an elaboration on the logic of privilege and responsibility, property and imperative, meaning and grammar, the same logic that modernity has struggled to resolve in the context of the tension between individual and group, private and public.

The centrality of such a logic is grounded and made explicit by the grammatical demarcation that has dominated virtually every language in the modern West, the one that has separated the singular from the plural and given to each a specific meaning and task. However, the advent of modernity is no more distinguished in its elaboration and championing of key ideological categories such as the autonomous subject than it is in its reconfiguration and historicization of the supposedly immutable structures of language. Indeed, many non-modern languages, such as Old English, Church Slavonic and Arabic, have imbedded in them the dual or the pair as a grammatical classification distinct from both the singular and the plural. What used to be the one, the two and the many as three distinct declensions of the noun has now given way to a linguistic, and by extension conceptual and cultural, not to mention psychological and economic, demarcation that separates the singular from the plural and the private from the public. Modernity's impact has been the quasi-eradication of the dual as a connection – 'this and that' – in favour of the dual as an oppositional and mutually exclusive disjunction 'either this or that'. While some traces of the former still persist in contemporary Slavic languages and in Hebrew, Arabic has refused to yield to the pressures of the modern. This might have much to do with that particular language's grammatical rootedness in the Koran as a religious text that has been held as sacrosanct and therefore immutable; I leave this question to the linguists and the historians.

The gradual disappearance of the dual as a connective declension has gone hand in hand with the rise of what have become the dominant ideological disjunctions self/other and individual/group, the same disjunctions that psychoanalysis has extended and translated into subject/object, reality/pleasure and eros/thanatos. The dropping of a declension is the dropping of a word, an object, an idea, a relation, an action and of all that they may entail. What we need to witness and account for in this process is no simple linguistic adjustment but, and much more radically, a transformation in being, in the ways it has been registered and consumed. It is precisely because psychoanalysis pursues its practice and production on the basis of words and their powers and through the free associations that are grounded in the dual as a connective mine and not mine that the discipline can be the most open to such a testimony.

As has become evident for the historians of ideas, Freud's elaborations on the unconscious, along with those of Marx on superstructure and Einstein on relativity, have counted among the principal forces behind the unsettling of the modern legacy of the subject as coherent and autonomous. What psychoanalysis has yet to articulate is a critique of those structures, psychodynamic, grammatical or otherwise, that have grounded that subject in its oppositional relation to the group and, by extension, the self to the other. I hardly wish to suggest that such an oppositionality is merely a linguistic by-product or that its treatment, should one choose to 'treat' it, is best achieved through a return to a pre-modern grammatical convention; nor am I claiming that it is merely a chimera that has little to do with the lived reality of both individual and group. My chief concern here is not with the dismantling or negation of modernity's legacy or of the maps of identity it has produced. Though hardly dead, such an identity is not the only thing that is alive and it need not always be alive in the same way. What interests me is the exploration of those spaces that modernity's maps cannot but miss, those positive spaces that we inhabit as transitional and transitioning subjects, and those excesses that the divide between self and other, individual and group cannot but overlook.

Clinically, while the picture we have often constructed has been focused on relations of conflict (between self and other) and/or deficit (suffered by the self on the hands of the other), we have overlooked a most significant dimension of the relationship that has little to do with either conflict or deficit. The subject that modernity has installed and that psychoanalysis has tried to unsettle is imbedded in a linguistic strategy that is neither static nor universal. Alongside it have resided other subjectivities that are more partial and localized, transitional connective subjectivities that have often been obfuscated by the rhetoric of identity and oppositionality but that have nonetheless retained their valence. Among the static peaks of rationality and universality one often crosses the local and dynamic crevices of tremor and desire. Through its use of free association, psychoanalysis is still one of the few practices suited for the uncovering of such crevices.

The ideological grammar of modern Western thought has helped that thought mark itself apart from all that has not paralleled it, be it other forms of thought which it dismisses as primitive or underdeveloped, or even, or should I say especially, parts of itself which it classifies as immature or pathological. However, and at its most potent and restrictive, modernity's grammar of opposites reinforces the notion that desire is a desire by the subject for an object; the subject desires what it does not have or more of what it already has, which amounts to the same thing. The subject is a subject in lack; it stands in opposition to the object as an object of consumption. As acquisition, such a desire is made to perpetuate and multiply the delineations between production and consumption, property and lack. While much is gained by a manoeuvre that emphasizes the subject and object in their separateness, the valence of the verb of desire not as a means of separation but as an existential and connective entity in its own right is almost entirely obfuscated. Sadly, psychoanalysis has fallen in step with such obfuscation.

Through the work of free association, the analytic transference provides us with a measure of counter-stability and openness in our dealings within modernity's logic of lack. The shared indeterminacy and ambiguity of the connective me and not me makes possible the agility of one's movement from one provisional subject-position to another, in-between such positions, and through them toward those that have yet to be articulated. There is hardly anything here that bespeaks the building or reinforcement of a predetermined structure that will supposedly help negotiate or improve one's relationships with objects, subjects and/or desires. There is much less of a proprietary logic, even if it be distributive and egalitarian, around knowledge or experience.

One of the principal effects of the logic of lack is that it reconfirms the occlusion of a space that is often presumed vacant and/or irrelevant. I am referring here to that space occupied by the verb in its unfolding, by the verb as a producing and a making present, and hence as an interrupting, without which the very idea of subject and object would be impossible. Consider, for instance, languages such as Arabic and Hebrew where, instead of the tripartite structure of 'subject-verb-object' with which we are most familiar, it is the deed, the doer, and the object upon which the deed is done that identify the principal components of the linguistic flow. Here, the doer cannot obtain unless the deed has already affirmed its position as leading.

It is the deed that produces the doer; the latter is not as easily assumed to choose whether or not to act the way it does; it is primarily the actant of the deed in question; it acquires its existence and identity through it.

In response to the theorists, psychoanalytic or otherwise, who have pinned desire to lack, I would like to redirect their attention to the times when they have analysed a dream, argued the intricacies of theory, danced, fucked, cooked a feast or listened to a story, to the tremors and passions particular to analysing, arguing, dancing, fucking, cooking or listening, the very same tremors and passions that have nothing to do with lack and everything to do with a doing. These theorists' resistance to an awareness of the doing, to the pursuit of its itineraries and productions, its presences and absences is what has held them pinned to the reifying logic of lack and consumption, means and ends, programs and categories.

Ultimately, one does not emerge from an analysis happier, stronger or clearer as to the truth of one's *jouissance*; one emerges more capable of a passionate mode of desiring that does not move one or happen to one, but a mode that is what one is and, in whatever degree, what one has always been, not as subject but as desiring. The passionate mode of desiring that is particular to an analysis is none other than free-associating. While necessary, the space and participation of the analyst are not ends in themselves; they are those catalysts and means that make it possible for the analysand to associate freely and to encounter the untimely-ness of his or her unconscious in the presence of another, and, in the process, to reinvest in a me and not me that is fundamentally altering of one's mode of being with others since the space of the untimely cannot be limited to the walls of a consulting room. All that I have been attempting thus far is an articulation of this verb of desire in its positive and unmediated presence. In order to highlight the fact that the individual on the couch is neither a patient nor a client but the one most presently and actively involved in the act of analyzing, the French borrowed from English the term analysand. In order to highlight the fact that desire is a present and active desiring, I would like to introduce the term désirand.

Notes

Chapter One

1 The literature on the Nietzsche-Freud connection is quite extensive; Jean-Michel Rey's *Parcours de Freud: Economie et discours* and Paul-Laurent Assoun's *Freud et Nietzsche* are excellent starting points.

2 The texts in question are, respectively, *Modern French Philosophy, The Myth of the Other, Deleuze and Guattari: An Introduction to Schizoanalysis* and *Deleuze et la psychanalyse.*

3 I have adopted the following abbreviations when quoting Nietzsche's texts: *BGE: Beyond Good and Evil*; *BT: The Birth of Tragedy; CW: The Case of Wagner*; *D: Daybreak*; *EH: Ecce Homo*; *GS: The Gay Science*; *HH: Human All Too Human*; *WP*: *The Will to Power*; *Z*: *Thus Spoke Zarathustra.* In most cases, references are indicated by aphorism number alone; chapter and section numbers and/or titles are included whenever appropriate.

4 To the ears of a Freudian, such thoughts should not sound too unfamiliar; after all, the ego is first and foremost a body ego.

5 Cf. Deleuze, *Nietzsche and Philosophy*, 39.

6 'Unspeakable' rather than 'not to be spoken;' this world is too exalted for the familiarity of words that level the unique and force it into the domain of the reproducible (*Z*, I, 5).

7 Cf. Lacan's 'The Function and Field of Speech and Language in Psychoanalysis' as well as Klein's 'The Importance of Symbol-Formation in the Development of the Ego' and Segal's 'Symbolism'.

8 Namely, *Twilight of the Idols, The Anti-Christ, Ecce Homo* and *Nietzsche Contra Wagner.*

Chapter Two

9 I have followed the standard practice of identifying phantasy as a phenomenon that is primarily unconscious in order to distinguish it from fantasy as the consciously willed work of the imagination.

10 See Sandler and Dreher's *What Do Psychoanalysts Want?* for an introduction to the debate and a historical survey of some of its main participants. Curiously absent from Sandler and Dreher's presentation is any reference to Lacan's problematizing contribution. For Lacan, the psychoanalyst's desire, what he or she 'wants', runs counter to 'the benevolent fraud of wanting-to-do-one's-best-for-the-subject' (*The Ethics of Psychoanalysis*, 219). Lacan asserts that, in order to make the drive present, the analyst's desire must not only tend in a 'direction that is the opposite

of identification' (*The Four Fundamental Concepts of Psychoanalysis*, 274), it must also be a desire to 'obtain absolute difference' (276). More than that of any of the other characters belonging to the psychoanalytic pantheon, Lacan's position here comes closest to Nietzsche's insistence on an unremitting dis-identification I discussed in the previous chapter. As we shall soon see, Lacan's shadow is never too far behind Deleuze and Guattari's use of that insistence.

11 Incidentally, it is the less than objective connotations of this conception that have grounded much of the twentieth century's critique of knowledge as the subject's attempt to eradicate otherness through its exercise of assimilation and control.

12 Norman Doidge's 'Empirical Basis for the Core Clinical Concepts and Efficacy of the Psychoanalytic Psychotherapies: An Overview' is a very useful introduction to the state of the research.

13 See John O'Neill's 'The Question of an Introduction: Understanding and the Passion of Ignorance'.

14 The likes of Frederick Crews, Jefferey Moussaieff Masson and Adolf Grünbaum come to mind.

15 This tension echoes the most singular opposition Freud had described first in 'The Unconscious' (206–7) and later in 'The Ego and the Id' (358–59) between a repressed unconscious thing presentation and a hypercathected pre-conscious word presentation.

16 For a more specifically feminist critique of this psychoanalyst-as-parent project, see Janice Doane and Devon Hodges' *From Klein to Kristeva: Psychoanalytic Feminism and the Search for the 'Good Enough' Mother.*

17 The list of readers and readings is formidable in its richness. See, among many others, Juliet Mitchell's *Psychoanalysis and Feminism*, her and Jacqueline Rose's introductions to *Feminine Sexuality*, Jessica Benjamin's *The Bonds of Love*, Joyce McDougall's *The Many Faces of Eros*, Julia Kristeva's *Black Sun*, and, last but not least, Teresa de Lauretis' *The Practice of Love.*

18 See his 'The Analytic Third: Working with Intersubjective Clinical Facts' and *Subjects of Analysis.*

19 See Elizabeth Roudinesco *Jacques Lacan & Co.*, 318–59.

20 See 'Mourning and Melancholia'.

21 Winnicott's approach here is radically different from that of other analysts who, under the influence of Melanie Klein, had also learned to appreciate the dynamics of projection and introjection. For instance, in his classic 'The Nature of the Therapeutic Action of Psycho-Analysis', James Strachey argued that the analysand's aggression is best treated by means of a series of mutative interpretations delivered by the analyst as auxiliary and benign, rather than disciplinary, super ego-like.

22 It seems as if Winnicott invokes this notion of the 'mature healthy adult' as a justification and a defence for what might otherwise be judged unjustifiable and indefensible. One imagines a scene in a higher court of clinical law where the psychoanalyst finds recourse in the legal standard of the 'reasonable man'. While an appeal to hypothetical reasonableness that represents the values and expectations of the community might sound, well, reasonable in matters of common law, one ought to be a bit reluctant to accord it the uncritical legitimacy Winnicott does in matters affective and psychodynamic.

[23] See note 17.

[24] Without lapsing into the quagmire of generational distinctions, Lacan attributes this passionate curiosity in part to the desire that is proper to the function of the analyst, e.g. as the driving force behind the process of analysis.

[25] In a modern Western cultural context, some have shown quite convincingly how homosexuality for instance has been as much of a taboo as incest; see on this score Eve Kosofsky Sedgwick's *Between Men* and *Epistemology of the Closet*.

[26] Jean Beaufret's analysis with Lacan for instance dates to as far back as the early 1950s; see Elizabeth Roudinesco *Jacques Lacan: Outline of a Life, History of a System of Thought*, 224.

[27] See his *The Tragic Effect*. In the early 60s, and long before Green, Levi-Strauss had already articulated this thought; see his *The Raw and the Cooked*, 48. For a clinical take, Leonard Shengold's *Soul Murder* and *Soul Murder Revisited* are highly insightful.

Chapter Three

[28] For *Anti-Oedipus*, all translations are mine; they will be indicated by *AO* followed by Fx for the page numbers of the French original then by Ey for the page numbers in the published English translation.

[29] This staccato is often completely lost in the English translation. I offer only three of, unfortunately, the many available examples:

1. *'Suite de la promenade du schizo, quand les personnages de Beckett se décident à sortir. Il faut voir d'abord comme leur démarche variée est elle-même une machine minutieuse'* (F8) is rendered 'Now that we have had a look at this stroll of a schizo, let us compare what happens when Samuel Beckett's characters decide to venture outdoors. Their various gaits and methods of self-locomotion constitute, in and of themselves, a finely tuned machine' (E2). The more accurate translation reads: 'Following the stroll of the schizo, when Beckett's characters decide to go out. See first how their varying walk is a meticulous machine' with the note that 'démarche' is as much a thought process as it is a physical movement.
2. *'Les Cahiers de l'art brut en sont la démonstration vivante (et nient du même coup qu'il y ait une entité du schizophrène)'* (F12) is rendered 'The *Cahiers de l'art brut* are a striking confirmation of this principle since by taking such an approach they deny that there is any such thing as a specific, identifiable schizophrenic entity' (E6); note here the introduction of a causal connection that does not obtain in the original. The translation should instead read: 'The *Cahiers de l'art brut* are living proof of this (as they simultaneously refute the fact of a schizophrenic entity).'
3. *'Antonin Artaud l'a découvert, là où il était, sans forme et sans figure'* (F14) is rendered 'Antonin Artaud discovered this one day, finding himself with no shape or form whatsoever, right there where he was at that moment' (E8); again, the more accurate translation should read 'Antonin Artaud discovered it, right there where it was, without form or figure.'

Repeatedly, the abruptness of the original text is smoothed by the published translation; its syntax is reconfigured and its phraseology padded.

30 Guattari went on to write a number of monographs, including *La révolution moléculaire*, *Les trois écologies*, *Chaosmose*, *Cartographies schizoanalytiques* and *Les années d'hiver*.

31 See Norgeu and Gentis' *La Borde: le château des chercheurs du sens?* for an account of the clinic and its workings.

32 Take, for instance, Elizabeth Roudinesco who lauds *Anti-Oedipus* as 'a great book' but only for its 'febrile syntax in which . . . the forgotten furor of a language of rapture and unreason comes to be couched'. Clinically, the book is as useful as Proust's *In Remembrance of Things Past* might be to someone looking for a 'story of maternal kisses and rosewater'; in fact, Roudinesco declares, *Anti-Oedipus* is a 'work filled with crude formulations, errors, and gross oversights' (*Jacques Lacan & Co.*, 496).

33 Note in this regard Serge Leclaire's assessment of the book's totalizing effect as a manoeuvre that dissipates all duality and, effectively, leaves the reader with the 'only prospect of being absorbed, digested, tied up and quashed' (Guattari, 'In Flux', 102).

34 One gets the impression that, for many admirers of Deleuze, *Anti-Oedipus* was, at best, a precursor to the presumably deeper and more thoughtful *A Thousand Plateaus*, or, at worst, an accidental distraction to be glossed over but never to be taken seriously. After an initial flurry of summaries and references, and but for the very few exceptions, the book seems to have disappeared from the secondary literature. Equally noteworthy in this context is the quasi-absence of any acknowledgement of Guattari's presence in the text, sometimes even as one of its two authors. 'In *Anti-Oedipus*, Deleuze writes . . . ' is a fairly common reference. I am not convinced that such attitudes reflect an accurate assessment of Guattari's contributions and/or intellectual merit. Rather, and in the case of the academic literature, my sense is that a censorship is at work here, a censorship whose object is much less the person of Felix Guattari and more so psychoanalysis as both a clinical practice and an intellectual endeavour. As for Guattari's absence from the clinically oriented texts, such as Monique David-Ménard's and Jean-Claude Dumoncel's, my hypothesis is that it may be a case of shunning, as only some analysts know how to do it.

35 The latter is Eugene Holland's interpretation (*Deleuze and Guattari*, 1–3).

36 In the spirit of such a tendency, and under the banner of a 'new' (!) nomadism, Rosi Braidotti has advocated a 'postpsychoanalytic' mode of theorizing the body ('Toward a New Nomadism', 1423). Meanwhile, Elizabeth Grosz has joined the ranks of those that are intent, yet again, on burying Freud – once and for all, of course. Grosz thus declares Teresa de Lauretis' *The Practice of Love* a failed and, she hopes, 'last attempt' ('The Labors of Love', 274) to account for female sexual desire from a psychoanalytic perspective. The failure for Grosz is constitutive of psychoanalysis itself; it is binding and comprehensive (292). Grosz sees no contradiction, let alone irony, in delivering an intellectual prohibition in the name of open-ended difference. For her part, de Lauretis finds the grace to conclude her response to Grosz's attack with the qualification that her book is addressed 'to whom it may concern' ('Habit Changes', 311).

[37] And hence as a form of thought rather than a condition or malady.

[38] This is a repeated motif in Deleuze. See, for instance, his comments on concepts that are suitable and texts that are useful (*Dialogues*, 3–4) and his declaration that 'theory is exactly like a box of tools. It has nothing to do with the signifier. It must be useful. And not for itself. If no one uses it, beginning with the theoretician himself (who then ceases to be a theoretician), then the theory is worthless or the moment is inappropriate' ('Intellectuals and Power', 208).

[39] Foucault writes: 'One must not look for a 'philosophy' amid the extraordinary profusion of new notions and surprise concepts; *Anti-Oedipus* is not a flashy Hegel. I think that *Anti-Oedipus* can best be read as an "art", in the sense that is conveyed by the term "erotic art" for example' (Preface, xii).

[40] In response to Foucault's query regarding his position on theory, Deleuze speaks of 'a system of relays within a larger sphere, within a multiplicity of parts that are both theoretical and practical . . . Representation no longer exists; there's only action – theoretical action and practical action which serve as relays and form networks' ('Intellectuals and Power', 206–7).

[41] François Dosse rightly labels this reification 'absurd' (*Biographie croisée*, 234). Dosse also points to the fact that Guattari would maintain a clinical practice with over 30 individuals well into the 1970s (223). Roudinesco also notes Guattari's status as a psychoanalyst in 1978 (*Jacques Lacan & Co.*, 498) and his continued membership in Lacan's *École Freudienne de Paris* around that same time (654) and hence long after his supposed renunciation of anything and everything psychoanalytic or Lacanian.

[42] One wonders as to why Deleuze and Guattari's professed choice must become their readers' prescription, especially since they themselves did not seem to be too concerned with upholding that choice. Their declarations in the text of the 1976 edition of *Rhizome* that they are 'tired' with psychoanalysis, that they found analysts and analysands 'too boring', and they would never again speak on the topic (*Rhizome*, 8) were undone only 2 years later as the references continued to multiply in *A Thousand Plateaus* and other texts. See also note 41.

[43] Here, Guattari's is a noticeably softer tone than the one Deleuze adopted in a number of post *Anti-Oedipus* texts; see, for instance, 'On the Vincennes Department of Psychoanalysis' where he and Jean-François Lyotard judged the discipline as a form of 'emotional and intellectual terrorism' (62) or 'Four Propositions on Psychoanalysis' where he charged the 'infamous art of interpretation' with 'crushing utterances, destroying desire' (85). However, it would be a bit too convenient to characterize Deleuze's stance as one-dimensional since one can also find comments from that same period that suggest an altogether different appreciation; see e.g. his flattering review of the psychoanalyst Pierre Fédida's *L'absence* in 'La plainte et le corps'.

[44] Dosse's *Biographie croisée* gives a most vivid account of this scene of writing. See especially pages 10–29 and 232–41.

[45] See Roudinesco *Jacques Lacan & Co.*, 495.

[46] See also *Psychanalyse et transversalité*, 72–85.

[47] 'In free associations [writes Adam Phillips] the patient takes the risk of not knowing what he is going to say' (*On Kissing*, 29). The same goes for listening, reading, and, indeed at times, writing.

[48] See Jacqueline Amati-Mehler et al.'s *The Babel of the Unconscious* for an excellent starting point.

[49] Nancy McWilliams' *Psychoanalytic Diagnosis* has become a classic on this issue.

[50] Twenty-five years after its first publication, Freud adds the following footnote to the penultimate chapter of *The Interpretation of Dreams*:

> I used at one time to find it extraordinarily difficult to accustom readers to the distinction between the manifest content of dreams and the latent dream-thoughts. Again and again arguments and objections would be brought up based upon some uninterpreted dream in the form in which it had been retained in the memory, and the need to interpret it would be ignored. But now that analysts at least have become reconciled to replacing the manifest dream by the meaning revealed by its interpretation, many of them have become guilty of falling into another confusion which they cling to with equal obstinancy. They seek to find the essence of dreams in their latent content and in so doing they overlook the distinction between the latent dream-thoughts and the dream-work. *At bottom, dreams are nothing other than a particular form of thinking made possible by the condition of the state of sleep. It is the dream-work which creates that form, and it alone is the essence of dreaming – the explanation of its peculiar nature.* (*The Interpretation of Dreams*, 649–50n2; emphasis added)

[51] Cf. Guy Debord's 'Theory of the Dérive'.

[52] Deleuze and Guattari's often referenced instance of this manoeuvre is Freud's reading of Schreber where everything is daddy: upper gods, lower gods, fathers and brothers.

Chapter Four

[53] It is worth noting here that Freud's most singular contribution to the study of the psyche was not the fact of the unconscious; mesmerists and hypnotists had already done that. Freud had posited the fact of a dynamic unconscious as a form of thought and a process, as in primary process, replete with its own set of procedures and formations (e.g. displacements, splits, defences and revisions) as the basis for his newly elaborated project.

[54] Here, Deleuze and Guattari adopt almost to the letter though, curiously enough, without proper accreditation, Marx's elaborations. See especially the second section of the *Grundrisse*'s Introduction entitled 'The General Relation of Production to Distribution, Exchange, Consumption' on pages 88–100. The *Grundrisse* had been available for a little over 20 years prior to the beginnings of the collaboration between Deleuze and Guattari. Marx had not intended his reflections for publication; they belonged to the personal notebooks he kept while preparing the three volumes of *Capital*.

Of particular relevance here is the fact that Marx was no less critical of naïve anti-Hegelianism than he was of the Hegelian logic without which his project would have been impossible. Marx managed to reformulate the debate in those materialist terms that have eluded the sensibilities of pro and con, pre and post.

The real is synchronous with thought, language, fantasy, and structure; as regards the quintessentially human, the filter of primacy, whether logical or chronological, loses its standing and primacy. Instead, Marx proposes an organic unity whose components are in constant mutual interaction, a unity that 'always returns to production, to begin anew' (99) as production, circulation, exchange and consumption. Rather than absolute identity (a thought that actualises itself in the real) or absolute opposition (a thought that cannot but surrender to the ineffability of the real), he insists on a thought fully aware of its status as part of the reality of which it speaks, a thought that hence participates in the dynamics it ascribes to its object (105).

55 John Austin's *How to Do Things with Words* on the 'performative' not only describing but producing that which it utters is quite useful.

56 Robert Castel is among the first to have endorsed this view: the concern of *Anti-Oedipus*, he argues, is not with any particular clinical technique or analytic experience but with the place of desire in the social field (*Le psychanalysme*, 271). Castel goes on to define schizoanalysis as a psychoanalysis that has been generalized: 'henceforth, the analytic fascination can be not so much broken as replayed and displaced, in the same way the subversion of Euclidian geometry's notion of space frees new spaces for the non-Euclidian geometries: in sum, a meta-analysis in the forth, social, dimension of desire' (273).

Castel's has in fact become the basic exegetical assumption for much of the literature on schizoanalysis. Massumi's *User's Guide* for instance concentrates on exposing the limits of a psychoanalytic approach for the broader understanding of desire while David-Ménard's *Deleuze et la psychanalyse* points to a turn in Deleuze's conceptual apparatus away from neurosis and schizophrenia and toward becoming and nomadism.

57 Three short texts by Jean-François Lyotard are worth consulting on this score: *Instructions Païennes*, *Tombeau de l'intellectuel* and *Les modes intellectuels*.

58 Among the most invoked of these are the mathemes of the four discourses: the hysteric's, the analyst's, the master's and the university's. See *On Feminine Sexuality: Seminar XX*, 16–17.

59 Derrida had already rejected Lacan's reading of the purloined letter on the ground that, of all the signifiers, 'Lacan' is the only one for whom the prerogative not to participate in the chain of sliding signifiers is retained. Protestations to the contrary notwithstanding, Lacan, the subject that is mistakenly supposed to know but ostensibly the subject that claims to know nothing, indeed knows much more that he is willing to admit, to himself as well as to others (see 'Le facteur de la vérité' in *The Postcard*). Lacan's response had already come 3 years prior to the publication of Derrida's critique; it consisted of the mathemes that, though they may serve the function of 'forms of language', do not constitute a meta-language (*On Feminine Sexuality: Seminar XX*, 118). After all, Lacan argued, no formalization of language is transmissible without the use of language itself. Consequently, there is no such thing as a meta-language, and Derrida's charge that the analyst had positioned himself as a meta-, i.e. as outside the circuit of letter exchange, is an error.

60 See the group's *Le cahier bleu* for its clinical and institutional blueprints.

61 One might even extend the scenario to the artistic domain and add, for instance, Picasso/Kandinsky to the list of couplets.

62 See especially the appendix on 'Plato and the Simulacrum' (253–66).

63 Many a post-Freudian reading has complicated our one-directional understanding of the tumultuous relationship between father and son. André Green for instance reminds us that Laius was not simply the innocent victim of patricide but the plotter of his own son's murder as well. In this context, much remains to be said of Jocasta's collusion with her husband's plot and of the ideological silence that surrounds that collusion to this day. Still, the structure and logic of the myth persist to the point where it has become virtually impossible to experience the familial, either phenomenally or ideologically, without its Sophoclean registering. However, and should art or history be our guide and inspiration, then let us not overlook the episode that Herodotus tells of Hippocrates who refused to abide by the prophecy's warning that he should not father a son or if he already has one to disown him. Pisistratus, his offspring, would go on to conquer Athens and serve as its ruler. Neither father nor son in this case was any the poorer for disregarding the codes of the deities and the directives of their prophets (*Histories*, Book One #59–64).

64 See his 'Sign Language Structure'.

65 See Oliver Sacks, *Seeing Voices*, 76.

66 See especially pages 691–700.

67 Deleuze writes:

> We all know ways of twisting the law by excess of zeal. By scrupulously applying the law we are able to demonstrate its absurdity and provoke the very disorder it is intended to prevent or to conjure. By observing the very letter of the law, we refrain from questioning its ultimate or primary character; we then behave as if the supreme sovereignty of the law conferred upon it the enjoyment of all those pleasures that it denies us; hence, by the closest adherence to it, and by zealously embracing it, we may hope to partake of its pleasures. The law is no longer subverted by the upward movement of irony to a principle that overrides it, but by the downward movement of humor which seeks to reduce the law to its furthest consequences. (*Coldness and Cruelty*, 88)

68 To render *jouissance* 'enjoyment' seems, to this reader at least, to disregard the term's critical status as a psychoanalytic category and, in the process, to divorce unjustifiably both the text and its authors from their intellectual surround.

69 Interestingly enough, and in order to make the identical claim, Deleuze and Guattari choose to invoke the authority of Marx on this matter (*AO*, F23, E16).

70 I am choosing to render the French '*je sens*' as 'I experience' instead of 'I feel', as per the English translation, in order to (a) underscore the physicality of the Deleuzo-Guattarian usage and hence (b) to distinguish it from the current preoccupation with 'feeling' in certain North American psychotherapeutic circles.

Chapter Five

71 It is worth noting here that such a working through is as much collective and cultural, considering the environment of concrete violence and destruction we inhabit, as it is psychodynamic and individual.

[72] Of course, to raise such a criticism against Deleuze and Guattari as I do against Freud, Klein and Lacan may sound unwarranted. Deleuze and Guattari have often advocated and, indeed, enacted the humorous in their texts and strategies. A wonderful illustration for Deleuze is his *Abecedaire* where, from 'Animal' to 'Wittgenstein', the philosopher's thoughts and gestures are often guided by wit and irony. Nevertheless, the authors of *Anti-Oedipus* remain anything but resolutely humourless in their condemnation of Oedipus.

[73] Incidentally, and if, in spite of all of this, some theatre-goers were still unaware of the plot and its outcome, they would have most likely treated the performance as much a detective mystery as a tragedy.

[74] See the entries dated 15 October '97, 5 November '97, and 15 March '98 in Masson's edition of the correspondence.

[75] Might there be a psychoanalytic import to the implicit homosocial contract between king and brother-in-law here?

Chapter Six

[76] See *The Interpretation of Dreams*, 649–50n2. See also 50 above note.

[77] The qualification here is that such representation is not readily available to consciousness; rather, it is the effect of a series of distortions, very much like in the dream work, that require interpretation; see Freud's 'Some General Remarks on Hysterical Attacks', 97–100.

[78] Reproductions of the paintings to which I refer in this chapter can be found at http://www.thepsychoanalyticfield.com/dgpi/

[79] See his 'The Patient as Therapist to His Analyst'.

[80] See his *Transference and Countertransference.*

[81] See his *The Shadow of the Object.*

[82] *Einstein, Picasso: Space, Time, and the Beauty that Causes Havoc.*

Chapter Seven

[83] My use of the term 'sexuality' here is not in reference to the identities invoked by the prefixes with which the word is often associated (hetero-, homo-, bi-, trans-, inter- . . .). My concern and emphasis are on the modes of sexuality rather than on the identificatory permutations of its subjects and objects, on the how rather than on the what or the who.

[84] Informed by the works of John Austin and Michel Foucault, Judith Butler and Eve Kosofsky Sedgwick were among the leading voices in the 1990s to have popularized this view; see Butler's *Gender Trouble* and *Bodies that Matter* as well as Sedgwick's 'Queer Performativity'.

[85] Whether this demand has always been genuine is an altogether different question.

[86] See *Exploits and Opinions of Dr. Faustroll*, 21.

[87] Geoffrey Cocks' *Psychotherapy in the Third Reich*, Regine Lockot's *Erinnern und Durcharbeiten* and Laurence Rickels' three-volume *Nazi Psychoanalysis* are quite informative on this score.

88 André Green captures the irreverence of this un-timeliness as a spark, and hence both a disruption and an illumination, in the title of one of his recent books *Le temps éclaté*.

89 Laplanche has written extensively on the dynamic of translation; see, among others, his 'Temporality and Translation', *Seduction, Translation, and the Drives* and *New Foundations for Psychoanalysis*.

90 As I have already argued near the end of the second chapter, the breakdown of chronology and the uncovering of the unconscious as untimely may occupy only a fraction of the time that is the frame of psychoanalysis; it is precisely within this fraction that the practice marks itself as singular and specific, as irreducible to this or that of the modes of relating with which we may be already familiar.

91 The rhetoric of relational integration and constancy has preoccupied a significant portion of the clinical literature recently. This rhetoric fails to address the fact that a quotient of irresolvable disagreement and antagonism sustains the clinical context. Sidney Blatt, for instance, speaks of a 'developmental transaction between relatedness and self definition' ('Representational Structures', 10) that is not simply an exchange but rather a complex interactive process between attachment and separation culminating in an integrated 'we' in which 'the capacity to cooperate and share with others is coordinated with a sense of individuality that has emerged from the development of autonomy, initiative, and industry' (13). Blatt's is not so much a harsh utopian ideal (harsh in the sense of unattainable and super-ego like, and hence punishing and retributive), but a misguided utopia of a 'we' that does not want to recognize the inevitability and even necessity of discord. One wonders how much of the 'self' is coerced into either acquiescence or oblivion in the name of such integration. One also wonders how much of integrity is compromised in the name of such integration, for integrity is precisely the ability to tolerate the truth of fragmentation even, and especially, at its most disrupting moments. Blatt will go on to speak of a 'personal and cultural relativism' as the marker of integration without really addressing the limits of said relativism when confronted with the absolute.

92 See, respectively, *The Preoedipal Origin and Psychoanalytic Therapy of Sexual Perversions, Male Homosexuality: A Contemporary Psychoanalytic Perspective*, and 'Defense Analysis in Self-Psychology: A Developmental View'.

93 This is indeed one of the principal arguments Winnicott builds throughout the essays that make up his *Playing and Reality*.

94 In a footnote to one of his discussions of the transference, Pontalis references an unpublished communication in which Michel Gribinski reminds us that *gegen* connotes proximity (*La force d'attraction*, 116). Gribinski infers here that the proper usage of the Freudian counter-transference requires that the analyst position him or herself alongside the analysand's transference and react to it. In positing this action–reaction sequence, Gribinski reconfirms, in his own fashion, the long-standing bias of attributing to the analysand the cause of, and hence the responsibility for, whatever in the analyst is not cognitive, diagnostic and interpretive, for, in other words, whatever is not measured, scientific. In some respects, this schema had already been taken up and elaborated by Daniel Lagache who, in his 'La méthode psychanalytique', identifies the transference and its

counter as cause and effect. What is interesting here is that Lagache was already convinced that the causal connection is not one-directional; indeed, transference and counter-transference belong to both analysand and analyst (as opposed to the one and the other respectively).

Bibliography

Aeschylus. *Seven Against Thebes* translated by H. H. Bacon. Oxford: Oxford University Press, 1973.

Amati-Mehler, Jacqueline, S. Argentieri and J. Canestri. *The Babel of the Unconscious: Mother Tongue and Foreign Languages in the Psychoanalytic Dimension* translated by J. Whitelaw-Cucco. Madison, CT: International Universities Press, 1993.

Aristotle *Poetics* in *Introduction to Aristotle* edited by R. McKeon. Chicago: University of Chicago Press, 1973. 662–713.

Assoun, Paul-Laurent. *Freud et Nietzsche.* Paris: Presses Universitaires de France, 1982.

Austin, John L. *How to Do Things with Words.* Oxford: Clarendon Press, 1975.

Bach, P. D. Q. *Oedipus Tex and Other Choral Calamities.* Telarc, 1990.

Bardi, Giovanni de'. 'Della tragedia'. Ms. C1. VII. 398, Biblioteca Nazionale Centrale, Firenze. Reprinted in *Per un regale evento* edited by M. Bartoli Bacherini. Firenze: Centro Di, 2000. 132–34.

Bateson, Gregory. 'Towards a Theory of Schizophrenia' in *Behavioural Science.* 1956:1. 251–64.

Beckett, Samuel. *Act Without Words I.* http://samuel-beckett.net/Act_Without_Words.html, accessed 6 May 2008.

Benjamin, Jessica. *The Bonds of Love.* New York: Pantheon Books, 1988.

Bion, Wilfred. 'Notes on Memory and Desire' in *The Psychoanalytic Forum.* 1967:2. 271–80.

Blatt, Sidney. 'Representational Structures in Psychopathology' in *Emotion, Cognition, and Representation, Rochester Symposium on Developmental Psychology* edited by Dante Cicchetti and Sheree L. Toth. Rochester: University of Rochester Press, 1995. 1–33.

Bollas, Christopher. *The Shadow of the Object: Psychoanalysis of the Unthought Known.* New York: Columbia University Press, 1987.

Bonnet, Marie-Jo. *Les deux amies.* Paris: Éditions Blanche, 2000.

Braidotti, Rosi. 'Toward a New Nomadism' in *Deleuze and Guattari: Critical Assessments of Leading Philosophers* edited by Gary Genosko. London: Routledge, 2000. 1414–39.

Burckhardt, Jacob. *The Civilisation of the Renaissance in Italy.* London: Phaidon Press, 1995.

Butler, Judith. *Bodies that Matter: On the Discursive Limits of 'Sex'.* New York: Routledge, 1993.

—. *Gender Trouble: Feminism and the Subversion of Identity.* New York: Routledge, 1990.

Castel, Robert. *Le psychanalysme: l'ordre psychanalytique et le pouvoir.* Paris: Flammarion, 1981. The first edition of this text appeared with Maspéro in 1973.

Cixous, Hélène. 'Savoir' in Hélène Cixous and Jacques Derrida *Veils* translated by Geoffrey Bennington. Stanford: Stanford University Press, 2001. 1–16. The original French text appeared in *Voiles*. Paris: Éditions Gallilée, 1989.

—. 'Tancredi Continues' in *Coming to Writing and Other Essays* edited by Debora Jenson with an introduction by Susan Rubin Suleiman. Cambridge: Harvard University Press, 1991. 78–103.

Cocks, Geoffrey. *Psychotherapy in the Third Reich*. Piscataway, NJ: Transaction Publishers, 1997.

David-Ménard, Monique. *Deleuze et la psychanalyse*. Paris: Presses Universitaires de France, 2005.

Debord, Guy. 'Theory of the Dérive' in *Situationist International Anthology* edited and translated by Ken Knabb. Berkeley: Bureau of Public Secrets, 1981. 50–54.

De Lauretis, Teresa. 'Habit Changes' in *differences*. 1994:6.2–3. 296–313.

—. *The Practice of Love: Lesbian Sexuality and Perverse Desire*. Bloomington: University of Indiana Press, 1994.

Deleuze, Gilles. *L'abecedaire de Gilles Deleuze* directed by Pierre André Boutang. Éditions Montparnasse, 2004.

—. *Coldness and Cruelty* translated by Jean McNeil in *Masochism*. New York: Zone Books, 1989. 7–138.

—*Difference and Repetition* translated by Paul Patton. New York: Columbia University Press, 1995.

—. 'Four Propositions on Psychoanalysis' in *Two Regimes of Madness*. 79–88.

—. 'Lettre à un critique sévère' in *Pourparlers: 1972–1990*. Paris: Les Éditions de Minuit, 1990. 11–23.

—. *The Logic of Sense* translated by Mark Lester and edited by Constantine V. Boundas. New York: Columbia University Press, 1990.

—. *Nieztsche and Philosophy* translated by Hugh Tomlinson. New York: Columbia University Press, 1983.

—. 'Nomad Thought' in *The New Nietzsche: Contemporary Styles of Interpretation* edited by David B. Allison. New York: Dell Publishing Co., 1977. 142–49.

—. 'On the Vincennes Department of Psychoanalysis' in *Two Regimes of Madness*. 61–62.

—. 'La plainte et le corps' in *Le Monde*, 13 October 1978.

—. *Two Regimes of Madness* edited by David Lapoujade and translated by Ames Hodges and Mike Taormina. New York: Semiotext(e), 2007.

Deleuze, Gilles and Michel Foucault. 'Intellectuals and Power' in *Language, Counter-Memory, Practice: Selected Essays and Interviews by Michel Foucault* edited with an introduction by Donald F. Bouchard. Ithaca, NY: Cornell University Press, 1977. 205–17.

Deleuze, Gilles and Felix Guattari. *L'anti-Œdipe*. Paris: Les Éditions de Minuit, 1973.

—. *Anti-Oedipus* translated by Robert Hurley, Mark Seem and Helen R. Lane with a preface by Michel Foucault. New York: Viking Press, 1977.

—. 'Capitalism and Schizophrenia' in Felix Guattari *Chaosophy*. 75–92.

—. *Kafka: Toward a Minor Literature* translated by Dana Polan. Minneapolis: University of Minnesota Press, 1986.

—. *Rhizome*. Paris: Les Éditions de Minuit, 1976.

—. *A Thousand Plateaus* translated by Brian Massumi. Minneapolis: University of Minnesota Press, 1987.

Deleuze, Gilles and Claire Parnet. *Diaologues* translated by Hugh Tomlinson and Barbara Habberjam. New York: Columbia University Press, 1987.

Derrida, Jacques. *The Postcard: From Socrates to Freud and Beyond* translated by Alan Bass. Chicago: University of Chicago Press, 1987.

Derrida, Jacques and Elizabeth Roudinesco. *De quoi demain*. Paris: Flammarion, 2001.

Descombes, Vincent. *Modern French Philosophy* translated by L. Scott-Fox and J. M. Harding. Cambridge: Cambridge University Press, 1980.

Doane, Janice and Devon Hodges. *From Klein to Kristeva: Psychoanalytic Feminism and the Search for the 'Good Enough' Mother*. Ann Arbor: University of Michigan Press, 1992.

Doidge, Norman. 'Empirical Basis for the Core Clinical Concepts and Efficacy of the Psychoanalytic Psychotherapies: An Overview' in *Standards and Guidelines for the Psychotherapies* edited by Paul Cameron, Jon Ennis and John Deadman. Toronto: University of Toronto Press, 1998. 80–142.

Dosse, François. *Gilles Deleuze et Félix Guattari: Biographie croisée*. Paris: Éditions la Découverte, 2007.

Dumoncel, Jean-Claude. *Le pendule du docteur Deleuze: Introduction à L'anti-Oedipe*. Paris: Epel Eds, 1999.

Euripides. *The Phoenician Women* translated by Peter Burian and Brian Swann. Oxford: Oxford University Press, 1981.

Fédida, Pierre. *L'absence*. Paris: Éditions Gallimard, 1978.

Foucault, Michel. *History of Sexuality: Volume 1 An Introduction* translated by Robert Hurley. New York: Random House, 1978.

—. 'Preface' in Deleuze, Gilles and Felix Guattari *Anti-Oedipus*. xi–xiv.

Freud, Sigmund. *The Pelican Freud Library* (referred to hereafter as *PFL*) under the general editorship of James Stratchey. Harmondsworth: Penguin, 1973–1986.

—. 'An Autobiographical Study' translated by Angela Richards in *PFL volume 15*. 183–259.

—. 'Beyond the Pleasure Principle' in *PFL volume 11*. 269–337.

—. 'The Ego and the Id' in *PFL volume 11*. 339–407.

—. 'On The History of the Psychoanalytic Movement' translated by Angela Richards in *PFL volume 15*. 57–128.

—. *The Interpretation of Dreams* translated by James Stratchey in *PFL volume 4*.

—. 'Mourning and Melancholia' in *PFL volume 11*. 245–68.

—. 'Psychoanalytic Notes on an Autobiographical Account of a Case of Paranoia' in *PFL volume 9*. 129–223.

—. *The Psychopathology of Everyday Life* translated by Alan Tyson and edited by Angela Richards in *PFL volume 5*.

—. 'Repression' in *PFL volume 11*. 139–58.

—. 'Some General Remarks on Hysterical Attacks' in *PFL volume 10*. 95–102.

—. 'Three Essays on the Theory of Sexuality' in *PFL volume 7*. 31–169.

—. *Totem and Taboo* in *PFL volume 13*. 43–224.

—. 'Two Encyclopaedia Articles' in *PFL volume 15*. 129–57.

—. 'The Unconscious' in *PFL volume 11*. 159–222.

Friedman, Richard. *Male Homosexuality: A Contemporary Psychoanalytic Perspective.* New Haven, CT: Yale University Press, 1988.
Green, André. *Le temps éclaté.* Paris: Les Éditions de Minuit, 2000.
—. *The Tragic Effect: The Oedipus Complex in Tragedy* translated by Alan Sheridan. Cambridge: Cambridge University Press, 1979.
Grosz, Elizabeth. 'The Labors of Love, Analyzing Perverse Desire: An Interrogation of Teresa de Lauretis's *The Practice of Love*' in *differences.* 1994:2–3. 275–95.
Guattari, Felix. *Les années d'hiver.* Paris: Éditions Barrault Bernard, 1986.
—. 'Beyond the Psychoanalytical Unconscious' in *Soft Subversions.* 192–201.
—. *Cartographies schizoanalytiques.* Paris: Éditions Galilée, 1989.
—. *Chaosmose.* Paris: *Éditions Galilée,* 2005.
—. *Chaosophy* edited by Sylvère Lotringer. New York: Semiotext(e), 1995.
—. 'Desire Is Power, Power Is Desire' in *Soft Subversions.* 15–23.
—. *Écrits pour l'anti-Œdipe* textes agencés par Stephane Nadaud. Paris: Éditions Lignes et Manifestes, 2004.
—. 'Everywhere at Once' in *Chaosophy.* 27–35.
—. *The Guattari Reader* edited by Gary Genasko. Oxford: Blackwell Publishers Ltd, 1996.
—. 'I Am an Idea Thief' in *Chaosophy.* 37–50.
—. 'In Flux' in *Chaosophy.* 93–117.
—. *Psychanalyse et transversalité.* Paris: Maspéro, 1972.
—. 'Psychoanalysis Should Get a Grip on Life' in *The Guattari Reader.* 69–73.
—. *La révolution moléculaire.* Paris: Union Générale d'Éditions, 1980.
—. 'Semiological Subjection, Semiotic Enslavement' in *The Guattari Reader.* 141–47.
—. *Soft Subversions* edited by Sylvère Lotringer and translated by David L. Sweet and Chet Wiener. New York: Semiotext(e), 1996.
—. 'So What?' in *Chaosophy.* 7–25.
—. 'The Transference' in *The Guattari Reader,* 61–68.
—. *Les trois écologies.* Paris: Éditions Galilée, 1989.
Herodotus. *Histories* translated by George Ravlinson with an introduction by Tom Griffith. Ware: Wordsworth Editions, 1996.
Holland, Eugene. *Deleuze and Guattari: An Introduction to Schizoanalysis.* New York: Routledge, 1999.
Homer. *The Iliad* translated by Robert Fagles. Harmondsworth: Penguin, 2003.
—. *The Odyssey* translated by Robert Fagles. Harmondsworth: Penguin, 2003.
Hvidberg, Flemming Friis. *Weeping and Laughter in the Old Testament.* Leiden: E. J. Brill, 1962.
Ionesco, Eugène. *La Cantatrice chauve suivi de La Leçon.* Paris: Éditions Gallimard, 1972.
Jarry, Alfred. *Exploits and Opinions of Dr. Faustroll, Pataphysician* translated by Simon Watson Taylor. Boston, MA: Exact Change, 1996.
Klein, Melanie. 'The Importance of Symbol-Formation in the Development of the Ego' in *Love, Guilt and Reparation and Other Works 1921–1945.* London: Virago Press, 1988. 219–32.
Klossowski Pierre. *Un si funeste désire.* Paris: Éditions Gallimard, 1963.
Kofman, Sarah. *Nietzsche and Metaphor* translated by Duncan Large. Stanford, CA: Stanford University Press, 1993.

Kristeva, Julia. *Black Sun: Depression and Melancholia* translated by Leon S. Roudiez. New York: Columbia University Press, 1989.

—. *New Maladies of the Soul* translated by Ross Guberman. New York: Columbia University Press, 1995.

Lacan, Jacques. *Ecrits* translated by Bruce Fink. New York: W. W. Norton & Company, 2002.

—. *The Ethics of Psychoanalysis. The Seminar of Jacques Lacan, Book VII* edited by Jacques-Alain Miller and translated by Denis Potter. New York: W. W. Norton & Company, 1992.

—. *The Four Fundamental Concepts of Psychoanalysis. The Seminar of Jacques Lacan, Book XI* edited by Jacques-Alain Miller and translated by Alan Sheridan. New York: W. W. Norton & Company, 1981.

—. 'The Function and Field of Speech and Language in Psychoanalysis' in *Ecrits*. 31–106.

—. *On Feminine Sexuality: The Limits of Love and Knowledge. The Seminar of Jacques Lacan, Book XX* edited by Jacques-Alain Miller and translated with notes by Bruce Fink. New York: W. W. Norton & Company, 1999.

—. 'The Subversion of the Subject and the Dialectic of Desire in the Freudian Unconscious' in *Ecrits*. 281–312.

Lagache, Daniel. 'La méthode psychanalytique' in Léon Michaux et al. *Psychiatrie*. Paris: Vrin, 1964. 1036–66.

Laplanche, Jean. *New Foundations for Psychoanalysis* translated by David Macey. Oxford: Blackwell, 1989.

—. *Seduction, Translation, and the Drives* a dossier compiled by John Fletcher and Martin Stanton. London: Institute of the Contemporary Arts, 1992.

—. 'Temporality and Translation' in *Stanford Literary Review*. 1989. 6:241–59.

Levi-Strauss, Claude. *The Raw and the Cooked* translated by John and Doreen Weighman. New York: Harper and Row, 1969.

Lockot, Regine. *Erinnern und Durcharbeiten: zur Geschichte der Psychoanalyse und Psychotherapie im Nationalsozialismus*, Frankfurt am Main: Fischer-Taschenbuch-Verlag, 1985.

Lutz, Tom. *Crying: The Natural and Cultural History of Tears*. New York: W. W. Norton & Company, 1999.

Lyotard, Jean-François. *Instructions Païennes*. Paris: Éditions Galilée, 1977.

—. 'Les modes intellectuels' in *Tombeau de l'intellectuel et autres papiers*. Paris: Éditions Galilée, 1984. 67–73.

—. 'Tombeau de l'intellectuel' in *Tombeau de l'intellectuel et autres papiers*. Paris: Éditions Galilée, 1984. 9–22.

Marx, Karl. *Capital* (3 volumes). Moscow: Progress Publishers, 1986.

—. *Grundrisse: Foundations of the Critique of Political Economy* translated with a foreword by Martin Nicolaus. Harmondsworth: Penguin, 1973.

Masson, Jeffrey M. *The Complete Letters of Sigmund Freud and Wilhelm Fliess*. Cambridge: Harvard University Press, 1985.

Massumi, Brian. *A User's Guide to Capitalism and Schizophrenia: Deviations from Deleuze and Guattari*. Cambridge, MA: MIT Press, 1992.

McDougall, Joyce. *The Many Faces of Eros*. New York: W. W. Norton & Company, 1995.

McWilliams, Nancy. *Psychoanalytic Diagnosis: Understanding Personality Structure in the Clinical Process.* New York: The Guilford Press, 1994.

Miller, Arthur I. *Einstein, Picasso: Space, Time, and the Beauty that Causes Havoc.* New York: Basic Books, 2001.

Mitchell, Juliet. 'Introduction – I' in *On Feminine Sexuality* edited by Juliet Mitchell and Jacqueline Rose. 1–26.

—. *Psychoanalysis and Feminism.* New York: Basic Books, 2000.

Mitchell, Juliet and Jacqueline Rose (eds). *Feminine Sexuality: Jacques Lacan and the école freudienne.* New York: W. W. Norton & Company and Pantheon Book, 1985.

Nietzsche, Friedrich. *Basic Writings of Nietzsche* translated and edited by Walter Kaufmann. New York: Random House, 1968.

—. *Beyond Good and Evil* in *Basic Writings of Nietzsche.* 179–435.

—. *The Birth of Tragedy* in *Basic Writings of Nietzsche.* 1–144.

—. *The Case of Wagner* in *Basic Writings of Nietzsche.* 601–53.

—. *Daybreak* translated by R. J. Hollingdale. Cambridge: Cambridge University Press, 1982.

—. *The Gay Science* translated with commentary by Walter Kaufmann. New York: Vintage Books, 1974.

—. *Ecce Homo* in *Basic Writings of Nietzsche.* 655–791.

—. *Human All Too Human* translated by Marion Faber with Stephen Lehmann. Linclon: University of Nebraska Press, 1984.

—. *The Portable Nietzsche* selected and translated by Walter Kaufmann. Harmondsworth: Penguin, 1983.

—. *The Anti-Christ* in *The Portable Nietzsche.* 565–656.

—. *Nietzsche Contra Wagner* in *The Portable Nietzsche.* 661–683.

—. *Thus Spoke Zarathustra* in *The Portable Nietzsche.* 103–439.

—. *Twilight of the Idols* in *The Portable Nietzsche.* 463–563.

—. *The Will to Power* translated by Walter Kaufmann and R. J. Hollingdale, and edited by Walter Kaufmann. New York: Random House, 1967.

Norgeu, Anne-Marie and Roger Gentis. *La Borde: le château des chercheurs du sens? La vie quotidienne à la clinique psychiatrique de La Borde.* Paris: Érès, 2006.

Ogden, Thomas. 'The Analytic Third: Working with Intersubjective Clinical Facts' in *International Journal of Psyhcoanalysis.* 75 (1994):3–19.

—. *Subjects of Ananlysis.* New York: Jason Aronson, 1996.

O'Neill, John. 'The Question of an Introduction: Understanding and the Passion of Ignorance' in *Freud and the Passions* edited by John O'Neill. University Park: Pennsylvania University Press, 1996. 1–11.

Partridge, Loren. 'Michelangelo's Last Judgement: An Interpretation' in *Michelangelo: The Last Judgement.* New York: Harry N. Abrams, 2000. 8–19.

Phillips, Adam. *On Kissing, Tickling, and Being Bored: Psychoanalytic Essays on the Unexamined Life.* Cambridge: Harvard University Press, 1993.

—. *Terrors and Experts.* Cambridge: Harvard University Press, 1995.

Pontalis, Jean-Bertrand. *Ce temps qui ne passe pas.* Paris: Éditions Gallimard, 1997.

—. *La force d'attraction: Trois essais de psychanalyse.* Paris: Éditions du Seuil, 1990.

Powers, Richard. *Galatea 2.2.* New York: Harper Perennial, 1996.

Quatrième groupe. *Le cahier bleu* in *Topique: Revue freudienne.* 1969:1. The text is also available online at http://quatrieme-groupe.org/pdf/le_cahier_bleu_3.pdf, accessed 6 May 2008.

Racker, Heinrich. *Transference and Countertransference.* New York: International Universities Press, 1968.

Rella, Franco. *The Myth of the Other: Lacan, Deleuze, Foucault, Bataille* translated by Nelson Moe. Washington DC: Maisonneuve Press, 1994.

Rey, Jean-Michel. *Parcours de Freud: Economie et discours.* Paris: Éditions Galilée, 1974.

Rickels, Lawrence. *Nazi Psychoanalysis* 3 volumes. Minneapolis: University of Minnesota Press, 2002.

Rose, Jacqueline. 'Introduction – II' in Juliet Mitchell and Jacqueline Rose, *On Feminine Sexuality.* 27–57.

Roudinesco, Elizabeth. *Jacques Lacan & Co.* translated with a foreword by Jeffrey Mehelman. Chicago: The University of Chicago Press, 1990.

—. *Jacques Lacan: Outline of a Life, History of a System of Thought* translated by Barbara Bray. New York: Columbia University Press, 1997.

Sacks, Oliver. *Seeing Voices: A Journey to the World of the Deaf.* Berkeley: University of California Press, 1989.

Sandler, Joseph and Anna Ursula Dreher. *What Do Psychoanalysts Want?* Foreword by Arnold Cooper. London: Routledge, 1996.

Searls, Harold. 'The Patient as Therapist to His Analyst' in *Tactics and Techniques in Psychoanalytic Therapy, Volume II: Countertransference* edited by Peter Giovacchini. New York: Jason Aronson, 1975. 95–151.

Sedgwick, Kosofsky Eve. *Between Men: English Literature and Male Homosocial Desire.* New York: Columbia University Press, 1985.

—. *Epistemology of the Closet.* Berkeley and Los Angeles: University of California Press, 1990.

—. 'Queer Performativity: Henri James's The Art of the Novel' in *GLQ.* 1993:1. 1–16.

Segal, Hanna. 'Symbolism' in *Dream, Phantasy and Art.* London: Routledge, 1991. 31–48.

Shengold, Leonard. *Soul Murder: The Effects of Childhood Abuse and Deprivation.* New York: Ballantine Books, 1991.

—. *Soul Murder Revisited: Thoughts about Therapy, Hate, Love, and Memory.* New Haven: Yale University Press, 2000.

Sloterdijk, Peter. *Thinker on Stage: Nietzsche's Materialism* translated by Jamie Owen Daniel with a foreword by Jochen Schulte-Sasse. Minneapolis: University of Minnesota Press, 1989.

Socarides, Charles. *The Preoedipal Origin and Psychoanalytic Therapy of Sexual Perversions.* Madison, CT: International Universities Press, 1988.

Sophocles. *Antigone* edited by Mark Griffith. Cambridge: Cambridge University Press, 1999.

—. *Oedipus at Colonus* translated by Eamon Grennan and Rachel Kitzinger. Oxford: Oxford University Press, 2005.

—. *Oedipus Rex* edited by R. D. Dawe. Cambridge: Cambridge University Press, 2006.

Steadman, Philip. *Vermeer's Camera: Uncovering the Truth Behind the Masterpieces.* Oxford: Oxford University Press, 2001.

Stokoe, William. 'Sign Language Structure' in *Annual Review of Anthropology.* 1980. 9:365–90.

Stone, Sandy. 'The Empire Strikes Back: A Post-Transsexual Manifesto' available online at http://sandystone.com/empire-strikes-back, accessed 6 May 2008.

Strachey, James. 'The Nature of the Therapeutic Action of Psycho-Analysis' in *The Evolution of Psychoanalytic Technique* edited by Martin S. Bergman and Frank R. Hartman. New York: Columbia University Press, 1990. 331–60.

Trop, Jeffrey and Robert Stolorow. 'Defense Analysis in Self-Psychology: A Developmental View' in *Psychoanalytic Dialogues.* 1992. 2:427–42.

Winnicott, Donald, W. 'Hate in the Conter-transference' in *Through Paediatrics to Psycho-Analysis: Collected Papers.* London: Hogarth Press, 1958. 194–203.

—. *Playing and Reality.* New York: Routledge, 1982.

—. 'The Theory of the Parent-Infant Relationship' in *The Maturational Process and the Facilitating Environment.* London: Hogarth Press, 1965. 37–55.

Index

CPSIA information can be obtained at www.ICGtesting.com
Printed in the USA
LVOW100049150113

315735LV00004B/54/P

9 781441 137784